Life may or may not have a reason, and many people have commented on it.

Here are some notable quotes that might shed some light.

Not all the answers are here, but there are plenty of interesting questions.

Ponder carefully and you might glimpse what it's all about.

Get this to people you know.

The only thing that does not change is everything changes.

Help that change happen.

http://dreamslaughter.com

Rear Cover Artwork: Keira Bossung

Cover Design: Jeffrey Abel

Burn This Book

selected quotes

By

dreamslaughter

dreamslaughter

P.O. Box 571454

Tarzana, California 91357

dreamslaughter

ISBN 10: 0-9771368-1-7

ISBN 13: 978-0-9771368-1-0

Library of Congress Control Number: 2005910150

BISAC Code: PHI000000

SAN: 2 5 6 – 7 9 3 8

This book is dedicated to everyone

The injury we do and the one we suffer are not weighed in the same scale.

~ *Aesop*

Any intelligent fool can make things better, more complex, and more violent. It takes a touch of genius, and a lot of courage to move in the opposite direction.

~ *Albert Einstein*

Experience is a hard teacher because she gives the test first, the lesson afterwards.

~ *Vernon Saunders Law*

The law, in its majestic equality, forbids the rich, as well as the poor, to sleep under the bridges, to beg in the streets, and to steal bread.

~ *Anatole France*

Insanity in individuals is something rare; but in groups, parties, nations, and epochs it is the rule.

~ *Nietzsche*

We must question the story logic of having an all-knowing all-powerful God, who creates faulty Humans, and then blames them for his own mistakes.

~ *Gene Roddenberry*

History is an account mostly false, of events mostly unimportant, which are brought about by rulers, mostly knaves, and soldiers, mostly fools.

~ *Ambrose Bierce*

Statistically one hundred percent of the shots you don't take don't go in.

~ *Wayne Gretsky*

What you do speaks so loud that I cannot hear what you say.

~ *Ralph Waldo Emerson*

Be happy while you're living, for you're a long time dead.

~ *Scottish proverb*

To be wronged is nothing unless you continue to remember it.

~ *Confucius*

Most of the things worth doing in the world had been declared impossible before they were done.

~ *Louis Brandeis*

Be kind; everyone you meet is fighting a hard battle.

~ *Unknown*

A thousand friends are few; one enemy is too many.

~ *Russian proverb*

That man is the richest whose pleasures are the cheapest.

~ *Henry David Thoreau*

I complained that I had no shoes until I met a man who had no feet.

~ *Persian proverb*

When great changes occur in history, when great principles are involved, as a rule the majority are wrong.

~ *Eugene V. Debs*

They made a wasteland and called it peace.

~ *Tacitus*

I contend that we are both atheists. I just believe in one fewer god than you do. When you understand why you dismiss all the other possible gods, you will understand why I dismiss yours.

~ *Stephen Roberts*

None are more hopelessly enslaved than those who falsely believe they are free.

~ *Johann Wolfgang von Goethe*

There is not one verse in the Bible inhibiting slavery, but many regulating it. It is not then, we conclude, immoral.

~ *Rev. Alexander Campbell*

I saw a human skull the other day. There was an inscription below it: 'Look long and hard at me, for I was once as you are and you will soon be as I am.'

~ *Unknown*

Kill a man, and you are an assassin. Kill millions of men, and you are a conqueror. Kill everyone, and you are a god.

~ *Jean Rostand*

There is no real wealth but the labor of man. Where the mountains are of gold and the valleys of silver, the world would not be one grain of corn the richer; not one comfort would be added to the human race.

~ *Percy B. Shelley*

Foreign aid is when the poor people of a rich country give money to the rich people of a poor country.

~ *Gary Hart, BC Comic Strip*

It is hard to free fools from chains they revere.

~ *Voltaire*

A lie can travel around the world while the truth is just putting on its shoes.

~ *Mark Twain*

The greatest artists of this world are never puritans, and seldom even ordinarily respectable.

~ *H. L. Mencken*

Every great advance in natural knowledge has involved the absolute rejection of authority.

~ *Thomas Huxley*

Everyone's values are defined by what they will tolerate when it is done to others.

~ *William Greider*

Football is a mistake. It combines the two worst elements of American life, violence and committee meetings.

~ *George Will*

If fifty million people believe a foolish thing, it is still a foolish thing.

~ *Anatole France*

Sports play a societal role in engendering jingoist and chauvinist attitudes. They're designed to organize a community to be committed to their gladiator.

~ *Noam Chomsky*

When you give food to the poor, they call you a saint. When you ask why the poor have no food, they call you a communist.

~ *Archbishop Helder Camara*

Knowledge comes, but wisdom lingers.

~ *Alfred, Lord Tennyson*

If you do not change direction, you may end up where you are heading.

~ *Lao tzu*

Christian is a VERB not a noun.

~ *Meria Heller*

How many legs does a dog have if you call the tail a leg? Four, calling a tail a leg doesn't make it a leg.

~ *Abraham Lincoln*

The beginning of wisdom is to call things by their right names.

~ *Chinese proverb*

He who knows nothing is closer to the truth than he whose mind is filled with falsehoods and errors.

~ *Thomas Jefferson*

I had a lover's quarrel with the world.

~ *Robert Frost*

Jesus isn't a philosopher in the epistemological sense. He's an adviser on how to live your life.

~ *<EmperorNorton>*

The believer is happy; the doubter is wise.

~ *Hungarian Proverb*

When science and the Bible differ, science has obviously misinterpreted its data.

~ *Henry Morris*

Written laws are like spider's webs; they will catch, it is true, the weak and poor, but would be torn in pieces by the rich and powerful.

~ *Anacharsis*

An upstart astrologer ... This fool wishes to reverse the entire science of astronomy; but sacred Scripture tells us that Joshua commanded the sun to stand still, and not the earth.

~ *Martin Luther on Copernicus*

Watching television is like taking black spray paint to your third eye.

~ *Bill Hicks*

If you've seen one Redwood tree, you've seen them all.

~ *Ronald Reagan*

We don't have to protect the environment; the Second Coming is at hand.

~ *James Watt, Reagan's Secretary of Interior*

It is better to teach knowledge one hour in the night, than to pray the whole night.

~ *Prophet Muhammad*

You cannot shake hands with a clenched fist.

~ *Indira Gandhi*

The people who have really made history are the martyrs.

~ *Aleister Crowley*

Laurel and Hardy, that's John and Yoko. And we stand a better chance under that guise because all the serious people like Martin Luther King, Jr. and Kennedy and Gandhi got shot.

~ *John Lennon*

Ye shall know the Truth, and the Truth shall make you angry!

~ *Aldous Huxley*

In the beginning there was nothing, which exploded.
~ Terry Pratchett

What do the nationalists say about killers punishing murderers and thieves sentencing looters?
~ Kahlil Gibran

An angry man opens his mouth and shuts up his eyes.
~ Cato

And I tell you, we are here on Earth to fart around, and don't let anybody tell you anything different.
~ Kurt Vonnegut

I meet the sincere man with sincerity and the insincere also with sincerity.
~ Lao Tse

Isn't it enough to see that a garden is beautiful without having to believe that there are fairies at the bottom of it too?
~ Douglas Adams

Philosophy is questions that may never be answered. Religion is answers that may never be questioned.
~ Unknown

Success is as dangerous as failure. Hope is as hollow as fear.
~ Tao Te Ching

A hushed heart hears the unuttered word.
~ Sri Aurobindo

Work like you don't need the money. Love like you've never been hurt. Dance like nobody's watching.
~ Satchel Paige

A man's ethical behavior should be based effectually on sympathy, education, and social ties and needs; no religious basis is necessary. Man would indeed be in a poor way if he had to be restrained by fear of punishment and hope of reward after death.

~ *Albert Einstein*

I would believe only in a god who could dance.

~ *Nietzsche*

... The CIA has overthrown functioning democracies in over twenty countries.

~ *John Stockwell, former CIA official*

If you can conceive of morality without god, why can you not conceive of society without government?

~ *Peter Saint-André*

It is not power that corrupts but fear. The fear of losing power corrupts those who wield it, and fear of the scourge of power corrupts those who are subject to it.

~ *Aung San Suu Kyi*

All that is human must retrograde if it do not advance.

~ *Edward Gibbon*

The forces in a capitalist society, if left unchecked, tend to make the rich richer and the poor poorer.

~ *Jawaharlal Nehru*

If you keep doing what you've always done, you'll keep getting what you've always gotten.

~ *Jim Rohn*

The trouble with the world is that the stupid are cocksure and the intelligent are full of doubt.

~ *Bertrand Russell*

We're going to fight in space, we're going to fight from space and we're going to fight into space... We'll expand into these two missions; space control and space force application, because they will become increasingly important. We will engage terrestrial targets someday, ships, airplanes, and land targets from space. We will engage targets in space from space.

~ *General Joseph Ashy, US Space Command's commander-in-chief, 1996*

On November 1, the General Assembly of the United Nations voted to reaffirm the Outer Space Treaty; the fundamental international law that establishes that space should be reserved for peaceful uses… Only two nations declined to support this bill, the United States and Israel.

~ *The Progressive magazine, January 2000, p27*

All movements go too far.

~ *Bertrand Russell*

If everything seems under control, you're just not going fast enough.

~ *Mario Andretti*

Like all dreamers, I mistook disenchantment for truth.

~ *Jean Paul Sartre*

The superior man thinks of virtue; the small man thinks of comfort.

~ *Confucius*

If we'd been born where they were born and taught what they were taught, we would believe what they believe.

~ *A church sign in Northern Ireland*

The corporation is a true Frankenstein's monster, an artificial person run amok, responsible only to its own soulless self.

~ *William Dugger*

Why tell me that a man is a fine speaker, if it is not the truth that he is speaking?

~ *Thomas Carlyle*

Hain't we got all the fools in town on our side? And ain't that a big enough majority in any town?

~ *Mark Twain*

In matters of conscience, the law of majority has no place.

~ *Mohandas Gandhi*

Let us overthrow the totems, break the taboos. Or better, let us consider them cancelled. Coldly, let us be intelligent.

~ *Pierre Trudeau*

Everything should be made as simple as possible, but not simpler.

~ *Albert Einstein*

Our scientific power has outrun our spiritual power. We have guided missiles and misguided men.

~ *Martin Luther King, Jr.*

We could have saved the Earth but we were too damned cheap.

~ *Kurt Vonnegut*

I've got to go to meet God, and explain all those men I killed at Alamein.

~ *Field Marshall Viscount Montgomery*

Life is like an overlong drama through which we sit being nagged by the vague memories of having read the reviews.

~ *John Updike*

The forceps of our minds are clumsy forceps, and crush the truth a little in taking hold of it.

~ *H. G. Wells*

It's not peace I want, not mere contentment; its boundless joy and ecstasy for me.

~ *Kugell*

A long and wicked life followed by five minutes of perfect grace gets you into Heaven. An equally long life of decent living and good works followed by one outburst of taking the name of the Lord in vain, then have a heart attack at that moment and be damned for eternity. Is that the system?

~ *Robert Heinlein*

Irrationally held truths may be more harmful than reasoned errors.

~ *Thomas Huxley*

In all affairs, it's a healthy thing now and then to hang a question mark on the things you have long taken for granted.

~ *Bertrand Russell*

Religion is not merely the opium of the masses; it's the cyanide.

~ *Tom Robbins*

In nature, there are neither rewards nor punishments; there are consequences.

~ *Robert G. Ingersoll*

You get what anyone gets; you get a lifetime.

~ *Death, Neil Gaiman Comic Sandman*

I object to violence because when it appears to do good, the good is only temporary; the evil it does is permanent.

~ *Mohandas Gandhi*

Convictions are more dangerous foes of truth than lies.

~ *Nietzsche*

I have the greatest admiration for your propaganda. Propaganda in the West is carried out by experts who have had the best training in the world, in the field of advertising, and have mastered the techniques with exceptional proficiency. Yours are subtle and persuasive; ours are crude and obvious. I think that the fundamental difference between our worlds, with respect to propaganda, is quite simple. You tend to believe yours and we tend to disbelieve ours.

~ *A U.S. based Soviet correspondent*

A terrorist is someone who has a bomb but can't afford an air force.

~ *William Blum*

A word to the wise is unnecessary.

~ *Francois Duc de la Rochefoucauld*

It does not do to leave a live dragon out of your calculations, if you live near him.

~ *J. R. R. Tolkien*

It does me no injury for my neighbor to say there are twenty gods, or no God. It neither picks my pocket nor breaks my leg.

~ *Thomas Jefferson*

It is the mark of an educated mind to be able to entertain a thought without accepting it.

~ *Aristotle*

All Bibles are man-made.

~ *Thomas Edison*

I cannot imagine a God who rewards and punishes the objects of his creation, whose purposes are modeled after our own; a God, in short, who is but a reflection of human frailty. Neither can I believe that the individual survives the death of his body, although feeble souls harbor such thoughts through fear or ridiculous egotisms...

~ *Albert Einstein, obituary*

Nothing overshadows truth so much as authority.

~ *Leon Battista Alberti*

In Christianity, neither morality nor religion comes into contact with reality at any point.

~ *Nietzsche*

Wisdom begins in wonder.

~ *Socrates*

I sometimes think that God in creating man somewhat overestimated his ability.

~ *Oscar Wilde*

I'm the one that has to die when it's time for me to die, so let me live my life, the way I want to.

~ *Jimi Hendrix*

Idealism increases in direct proportion to one's distance from the problem.

~ *John Galsworthy*

If English was good enough for Jesus, it's good enough for them Mexicans.

~ *Texas politician, Spanish as a second language*

No one rules if no one obeys.

~ *<TaoDo>*

A language is a dialect with an army and a navy.

~ *Max Weinreich*

It is dangerous to be right in matters on which the established authorities are wrong.

~ *Voltaire*

Beware of the man whose god is in the skies.

~ *George Bernard Shaw*

Almost all absurdity of conduct arises from the imitation of those whom we cannot resemble.

~ *Samuel Johnson*

We have just enough religion to make us hate, but not enough to make us love one another.

~ *Jonathan Swift*

If you ever drop your keys into a river of molten lava, let 'em go, because, man, they're gone.

~ *Jack Handey*

America is a large friendly dog in a small room. Every time it wags its tail it knocks over a chair.

~ *Arnold Toynbee*

I think it would be totally inappropriate for me to even contemplate what I am thinking about.

~ *Don Mazankowski*

First, they ignore you. Then they laugh at you. Then they fight you. Then you win.

~ *Mohandas Gandhi*

... It is important to realize that any lock can be picked with a big enough hammer.

~ *Sun System & Network Admin manual*

Almost all our faults are more pardonable than the methods we resort to hide them.

~ *Francois Duc de la Rochefoucauld*

A fanatic is one who can't change his mind and won't change the subject.

~ *Winston Churchill*

A good programmer is someone who looks both ways before crossing a one-way street.

~ *Doug Linder*

A lady is always grateful for a sincere compliment, so long as you don't try to knock her down with it.

~ *Mark Twain*

The crimes of the U.S. throughout the world have been systematic, constant, clinical, remorseless, and fully documented but nobody cares to talk about them.

~ *Harold Pinter*

A great many people think they are thinking when they are merely rearranging their prejudices.

~ *William James*

We always obeyed the law. Isn't that what you do in America? Even if you don't agree with a law personally, you still obey it. Otherwise life would be chaos.

~ *Gertrude Scholtz-Klink, explaining Nazi policy*

To sin by silence when they should protest makes cowards of men.

~ *Abraham Lincoln*

I am strongly in favor of using poisoned gas against uncivilized tribes. The moral effect should be good and it would spread a lively terror.

~ *Winston Churchill commenting on the British use of poison gas against the Iraqis after World War I*

... Somehow we find it hard to sell our values, namely that the rich should plunder the poor.

~ *John Foster Dulles*

The target suffered a terminal illness before a firing squad in Baghdad.

~ *CIA officer at US Senate hearing on 1963 overthrow of Iraqi Prime Minister Kassem*

Under capitalism, man exploits man. Under communism, it's just the opposite.

~ *John Kenneth Galbraith*

Terrorists are just Freedom Fighters pointed back at us.

~ *Michael Rivero*

Don't try to teach a pig to sing, it can't be done and it only ticks off the pig.

~ *Robert Heinlein*

Form no covetous desire, so that the demon of greediness may not deceive thee, and the treasure of the world may not be tasteless to thee.

~ *Zoroaster*

In every country and every age, the priest has been hostile to liberty.

~ *Thomas Jefferson*

Faced with the choice between changing one's mind and proving that there is no need to do so, almost everyone gets busy on the proof.

~ *Galbraith's Law*

A celibate clergy is an especially good idea, because it tends to suppress any hereditary propensity toward fanaticism.

~ *Carl Sagan*

Our government has kept us in a perpetual state of fear, kept us in a continuous stampede of patriotic fervor, with the cry of grave national emergency. Always there has been some terrible evil at home or some monstrous foreign power that was going to gobble us up if we did not blindly rally behind it.

~ *General Douglas MacArthur*

A short saying oft contains much wisdom.

~ *Sophocles*

A halo has to fall only a few inches to become a noose.

~ *Farmers Almanac*

I am amazed how many people on this planet are happy and free and never even saw the US constitution.

~ *<Reason>*

Authoritarian government required to speak, is silent. Representative government required to speak, lies with impunity.

~ *Napoleon*

All philosophies and religions are but partial truths. One must meld them together to arrive at greater truths.

~ *Shawn Mikula*

Men who are orthodox when they are young are in danger of being middle aged all their lives.

~ *Walter Lippmann*

The absurd man is one who never changes.

~ *Auguste Barthelemy*

Talent does what it can; genius does what it must.

~ *Edward George Bulwer-Lytton*

The last Christian died on the cross.

~ *Nietzsche*

The more laws and order are made prominent, the more thieves and robbers there will be.

~ *Lao Tsu*

People with virtue must speak out; People who speak are not all virtuous.

~ *Confucius*

Superior and alone, Confucius stood, who taught that useful science, to be good.

~ *Alexander Pope*

Write on my gravestone: Infidel, traitor, and infidel to every church that compromises with wrong; traitor to every government that oppresses the people.

~ *Wendell Phillips*

The first clergyman was the first rascal who met the first fool.

~ *Voltaire*

The philosopher has never killed any priests, whereas the priest has killed a great many philosophers.

~ *Denis Diderot*

When you have to kill a man, it costs nothing to be polite.

~ *Winston Churchill*

One death is a tragedy. A million deaths is a statistic.

~ *Josef Stalin*

When liberty is taken away by force it can be restored by force. When it is relinquished voluntarily by default, it can never be recovered.

~ *Dorothy Thompson*

It is not by the sword or the spear, by soldiers or by armed force that truth is to be promoted, but by counsel and gentle persuasion.

~ *Saint Athenasius*

Kindness in words creates confidence. Kindness in thinking creates profoundness. Kindness in giving creates love.

~ *Lao tzu*

Problems cannot be solved at the same level of awareness that created them.

~ *Albert Einstein*

The least initial deviation from the truth is multiplied later a thousand fold.

~ *Aristotle*

We can often do more for other men by trying to correct our own faults than by trying to correct theirs.

~ *Francois Fenelon*

Be the change that you want to see in the world.
~ *Mohandas Gandhi*

All wisdom lies in temperance, tolerance and charity.
~ *Zarathushtra*

Demagogue: One who preaches a doctrine he knows to be untrue to men he knows to be idiots.
~ *H. L. Mencken*

Peace is over rated. Any slave can have peace. Just pick the cotton.
~ *TheSong*

Avarice: the spur of industry.
~ *David Hume*

We may know that there are five essentials for victory: 1) He will win who knows when to fight and not to fight. 2) He will win who knows how to handle both superior and inferior forces. 3) He will win whose army is animated by the same spirit throughout all the ranks. 4) He will win who, prepared himself, waits to take the enemy unprepared. 5) He will win who has military capacity and is not interfered with by his sovereign. Victory lies in the knowledge of these five points.
~ *Sun tzu*

A man never tells you anything until you contradict him.
~ *George Bernard Shaw*

News is what someone wants to suppress. Everything else is advertising.
~ *Ex-NBC news president Rubin Frank*

Nothing is too much trouble.
~ *Edward Kirby Bonds*

The greatest discovery of my generation is that man can alter his life simply by altering his attitude of mind.
~ *William James*

For every minute you are angry you lose sixty seconds of happiness.
~ *Ralph Waldo Emerson*

The stoical scheme of supplying our wants by lopping off our desires is like cutting off our feet when we want shoes.
~ *Jonathan Swift*

When women are depressed they either eat or go shopping. Men invade another country.
~ *Elayne Boosler*

The superior man understands what is right; the inferior man understands what will sell.
~ *Confucius*

The pure and simple truth is rarely pure and never simple.
~ *Oscar Wilde*

To use the term blind faith, is to use an adjective needlessly.
~ *Julian Ruck*

The study of the Confucian philosophy is of greater profit than that of Greek.
~ *Ezra Pound*

It is right noble to fight with wickedness and wrong; the mistake is in supposing that spiritual evil can be overcome by physical means.
~ *Lydia Maria Child*

Nothing except a battle lost can be half as melancholy as a battle won.

~ *Duke of Wellington*

The only way to abolish war is to make peace heroic.

~ *John Dewey*

All warfare is based on deception.

~ *Sun tzu*

We need a common enemy to unite us.

~ *Condoleezza Rice, March 2000*

Nothing brings people together more, than mutual hatred.

~ *Henry Rollins*

Everyone thinks of changing the world, but no one thinks of changing himself.

~ *Leo Tolstoy*

Be careful of your thoughts, for your thoughts become your words. Be careful of your words, for your words become your actions. Be careful of your actions, for your actions become your habits. Be careful of your habits, for your habits become your character. Be careful of your character, for your character becomes your destiny.

~ *Unknown*

The journey is the reward.

~ *Chinese Proverb*

Let us read the Bible without the ill-fitting colored spectacles of theology, just as we read other books, using our judgment and reason.

~ *Luther Burbank*

To be matter of fact about the world is to blunder into fantasy and dull fantasy at that, as the real world is strange and wonderful.

~ *Robert Heinlein*

You see a lot of smart guys with dumb women, but you hardly ever see a smart woman with a dumb guy.

~ *Erica Jong*

Love is perfect kindness.

~ *Joseph Campbell*

Computers are useless. They can only give you answers.

~ *Pablo Picasso*

Democracy is four wolves and a lamb voting on what to have for lunch.

~ *Ambrose Bierce*

The less government we have the better.

~ *Ralph Waldo Emerson*

You simply cannot hang a millionaire in America.

~ *Bourke Cockran*

History is a joke played by the victors on the vanquished in front of an audience that dares not laugh.

~ *Michael Rivero*

The compulsion to do good is an innate American trait. Only North Americans seem to believe that they always should, may, and actually can choose somebody with whom to share their blessings. Ultimately this attitude leads to bombing people into the acceptance of gifts.

~ *Ivan Illich*

Reality can destroy the dream; why shouldn't the dream destroy reality?

~ *George Moore*

Just as a picture is drawn by an artist, surroundings are created by the activities of the mind.

~ *Buddha*

The best way to make children good is to make them happy.

~ *Oscar Wilde*

The minority, the ruling class at present, has the schools and press, usually the Church as well under its thumb. This enables it to organize and sway the emotions of the masses, and make its tool of them.

~ *Albert Einstein*

A man who lost his axe suspected his neighbor's son of stealing it. To him, as he observed the boy, the way the lad walked; the expression on his face, the manner of his speech; in fact everything about his appearance and behavior betrayed that he had stolen the axe. Not long afterwards the man found his axe while digging in his cellar. When he saw his neighbor's son again, nothing about the boy's behavior or appearance seemed to suggest that he had stolen the axe.

~ *Liezi*

Failure is the opportunity to begin again more intelligently.

~ *Henry Ford*

Say what you will about the sweet miracle of unquestioning faith. I consider the capacity for it terrifying.

~ *Kurt Vonnegut*

We hang the petty thieves and appoint the great ones to public office.

~ *Aesop*

In the 1980s capitalism triumphed over communism. In the 1990s it triumphed over democracy.

~ *David Korten*

All civilization has from time to time become a thin crust over a volcano of revolution.

~ *Havelock Ellis*

Rewards and punishments are the lowest form of education.

~ *Chuang tzu*

Every gun that is made, every warship launched, every rocket fired signifies in the final sense, a theft from those who hunger and are not fed, those who are cold and are not clothed. This world in arms is not spending money alone. It is spending the sweat of its laborers, the genius of its scientists, the hopes of its children. This is not a way of life at all in any true sense. Under the clouds of war, it is humanity hanging on a cross of iron.

~ *Dwight D. Eisenhower*

Borrow trouble for yourself, if that's your nature, but don't lend it to your neighbors.

~ *Rudyard Kipling*

We can do no great things; only small things with great love.

~ *Mother Teresa*

If you speak the truth, have one foot in the stirrup.

~ *Turkish proverb*

We choose our joys and sorrows long before we experience them.

~ *Kahlil Gibran*

Knowledge, idea, belief stands in the way of wisdom.

~ *J. Krishnamurthi*

Intolerance is evidence of impotence.

~ *Aleister Crowley*

Git yer guns, the liberal folks are gonna let the coloreds vote!

~ *Unknown*

Outside of the killings, Washington has one of the lowest crime rates in the country.

~ *Marion Barry, former mayor Washington D.C.*

Seek not happiness too greedily, and be not fearful of unhappiness.

~ *Lao tzu*

Only the wisest and stupidest of men never change.

~ *Confucius*

Make haste slowly.

~ *Emperor Augustus*

When I told the people of Northern Ireland that I was an atheist, a woman in the audience stood up and said, 'Yes, but is it the God of the Catholics or the God of the Protestants in whom you don't believe?'

~ *Quentin Crisp*

Isn't it pathetic that we can fuck but we can't look each other in the eyes?

~ *Henry Rollins*

The darkest places in hell are reserved for those who remain neutral in times of moral crisis.

~ *Dante*

Whatever the natural cause, sin is the true cause of all earthquakes.

~ *John Wesley*

Jehovah was not a moral god. He had all the vices and he lacked all the virtues. He generally carried out all his threats, but he never faithfully kept a promise.

~ *Robert G. Ingersoll*

I am not sure that God always knows who his great men are; he is so very careless of what happens to them while they live.

~ *Mary Hunter Austin*

Anyone who has two shirts when someone has none is not a Christian.

~ *Lenny Bruce*

When the people fear the government you have tyranny; when the government fears the people you have liberty.

~ *Thomas Jefferson*

To every action there is always opposed an equal reaction.

~ *Sir Isaac Newton*

Getting what you go after is success; but liking it while you are getting it is happiness.

~ *Bertha Damon*

All thinking men are atheists.

~ *Ernest Hemingway*

The cannon thunders... limbs fly in all directions... one can hear the groans of victims and the howling of those performing the sacrifice... it's humanity in search of happiness.

~ *Charles Baudelaire*

If there has to be a blood bath, let's get it over with.

~ *Ronald Reagan, Vietnam*

If we could read the secret history of our enemies, we should find in each man's life sorrow and suffering enough to disarm all hostility.

~ *Henry Wadsworth Longfellow*

In seeking wisdom, thou art wise; in imagining that thou has attained it, thou art a fool.

~ *Simon Ben Azzai*

Man is certainly stark mad: he cannot make a worm, yet he will make gods by the dozen.

~ *Michel de Montaigne*

A casual stroll through the lunatic asylum shows that faith does not prove anything.

~ *Nietzsche*

I read about an Eskimo hunter who asked the local missionary priest, 'If I did not know about God and sin, would I go to hell?'
'No,' said the priest, 'not if you did not know.'
'Then why,' asked the Eskimo earnestly, 'did you tell me?'

~ *Annie Dillard*

To surrender to ignorance and call it god has always been premature, and it remains premature today.

~ *Isaac Asimov*

If an historian were to relate truthfully all the crimes, weaknesses and disorders of mankind, his readers would take his work for satire rather than for history.

~ *Pierre Bayle*

I am convinced that I am acting as the agent of our Creator. By fighting off the Jews, I am doing the Lord's work.

~ *Adolf Hitler*

[In outer space] you develop an instant global consciousness, a people orientation, an intense dissatisfaction with the state of the world, and a compulsion to do something about it. From out there on the moon, international politics look so petty. You want to grab a politician by the scruff of the neck and drag him a quarter of a million miles out and say, 'Look at that, you son of a bitch'

~ *Edgar Mitchell*

Generosity is not giving me that which I need more than you do, but it is giving me that which you need more than I do.

~ *Kahlil Gibran*

He who knows that enough is enough will always have enough.

~ *Lao Tsu*

At the age of eleven or thereabouts women acquire a poise and an ability to handle difficult situations which a man, if he is lucky, manages to achieve somewhere in the later seventies.

~ *P. G. Wodehouse*

Quick decisions are unsafe decisions.

~ *Sophocles*

Unless one has mastered these three things, desire for power, desire for money, and desire for sex, one cannot possess any of them firmly and surely.

~ *The Mother Mirra*

You exist only in what you do.

~ *Federico Fellini*

I was working on the proof of one of my poems all the morning, and took out a comma. In the afternoon I put it back again.

~ *Oscar Wilde*

Missionaries are perfect nuisances and leave every place worse than they found it.

~ *Charles Dickens*

Art has to be forgotten; beauty must be realized.

~ *Piet Mondrian*

Peace is not merely the absence of war. It is also a state of mind. Lasting peace can come only to peaceful people.

~ *Jawaharlal Nehru*

A fool who is conscious of his folly is thereby wise; the fool who thinks himself wise is the one to be called a fool.

~ *Dhammapada*

I know nothing except the fact of my ignorance.

~ *Socrates*

A violent act pierces the atmosphere, leaving a hole through which the cold, damp draft of its memory blows forever.

~ *Jane Stanton Hitchcock*

Religion is regarded by the common people as true, by the wise as false, and by rulers as useful.

~ *Seneca the Younger*

All truth passes through three stages. First, it is ridiculed. Second, it is violently opposed. Third, it is accepted as being self-evident.

~ *Arthur Schopenhauer*

No country has suffered so much from the ruins of war while being at peace as the American.

~ *Edward Dahlberg*

Kindness is more important than wisdom, and the recognition of this is the beginning of wisdom.

~ *Theodore Isaac Rubin*

Truth isn't always beauty, but the hunger for it is.

~ *Nadine Gordimer*

You can't say civilizations don't advance, because they kill you in a new way in each war.

~ *Will Rogers*

It is not so much the suffering as the senselessness of it that is unendurable.

~ *Nietzsche*

Each nation knowing it has the only true religion and the only sane system of government, each despising all the others, each an ass and not suspecting it.

~ *Mark Twain*

To assert that the earth revolves around the sun is as erroneous as to claim that Jesus was not born of a virgin.

~ *Cardinal Bellarmine, the trial of Galileo*

Darkness cannot drive out darkness; only light can do that. Hate cannot drive out hate; only love can do that.

~ *Martin Luther King, Jr.*

If it were all so simple! If only there were evil people somewhere insidiously committing evil deeds, and it were necessary only to separate them from the rest of us and destroy them; but the line dividing good and evil cuts through the heart of every human being. And who is willing to destroy a piece of his own heart?

~ *Aleksandr Solzhenitsyn*

Even a god cannot change the past.

~ *Agathon*

We hold truths that all men are created equal, that they are endowed by their Creator with certain unalienable rights, among these are life, liberty and the pursuit of happiness.

~ *Ho Chi Minh, 1945, as the Democratic Republic of Vietnam was created*

In order to be an immaculate member of a flock of sheep, one must above all be a sheep oneself.

~ *Albert Einstein*

The church tries to save sinners, but science seeks to stop their manufacture.

~ *Elbert Hubbard*

I can't embrace a male god who has persecuted female sexuality throughout the ages; and that persecution still goes on today, all over the world.

~ *Amanda Donohoe*

Any fool can make a rule, and any fool will mind it.

~ *Henry David Thoreau*

What is most beautiful in virile men is something feminine; what is most beautiful in feminine women is something masculine.

~ *Susan Sontag*

Pontius Pilate was the first great censor, and Jesus Christ the first great victim of censorship.

~ *Ben Lindsay*

The whole history of the last thousands of years has been a history of religious persecutions and wars, pogroms, jihads, crusades. I find it all very regrettable.

~ *Steven Weinberg*

You will kill ten of our men, and we will kill one of yours, and in the end it will be you who tire of it.

~ *Ho Chi Minh*

People do strange things when they are cornered by facts. When evidence cannot be denied, men who care nothing for the truth simply become illogical. Minds become willfully ignorant and emotions turn hostile.

~ *Richard Sisson*

We are what we think. All that we are arises with our thoughts. With our thoughts, we make the world.

~ *Buddha*

It is lamentable, that to be a good patriot one must become the enemy of the rest of mankind.

~ *Voltaire*

Few people are capable of expressing with equanimity opinions which differ from the prejudices of their social environment. Most people are even incapable of forming such opinions.

~ *Albert Einstein*

I thought dying for your country was the worst thing that could happen to you. I think killing for your country can be a lot worse; because that's the memory that haunts.

~ *Bob Kerry told to The New York Times*

Contraction of theological influence has at once been the best measure, and the essential condition of intellectual advance.

~ *William H. Lecky*

Isn't killing people in the name of God a pretty good definition of insanity?

~ *Arthur C. Clarke*

Most of us spend too much time on the last twenty-four hours and too little on the last six thousand years.

~ *Will Durant*

Liberty is the only thing you cannot have unless you are willing to give it to others.

~ *William Allen White*

Talent hits a target no one else can hit; Genius hits a target no one else can see.

~ *Arthur Schopenhauer*

Oh Mortal Man, is there nothing you cannot be made to believe?

~ *Adam Weishaupt, Co-founder New World Order*

Do not speak ill of the dead.

~ *The Seven Sages*

There are three truths: my truth, your truth, and the truth.

~ *Chinese proverb*

I have recently been examining all the known superstitions of the world, and do not find in our particular superstition [Christianity] one redeeming feature. They are all alike, founded upon fables and mythologies.

~ *Thomas Jefferson*

The most heinous and the cruelest crimes of which history has record have been committed under the cover of religion or equally noble motives.

~ *Mohandas Gandhi*

The road up and the road down are one and the same.

~ *Heraclitus*

It is the province of knowledge to speak, and it is the privilege of wisdom to listen.

~ *Oliver Wendell Holmes*

We are not retreating; we are advancing in another direction.

~ *General Douglas MacArthur*

Another such victory and we are undone.

~ *Pyrrhus*

I don't know what I may seem to the world, but as to myself, I seem to have been only like a boy playing on the seashore and diverting myself in now and then finding a smoother pebble or a prettier shell than ordinary, whilst the great ocean of truth lay all undiscovered before me.

~ *Sir Isaac Newton*

Soap and education are not as sudden as a massacre, but they are more deadly in the long run.

~ *Mark Twain*

Either God wants to abolish evil, and cannot; or he can, but does not want to. If he wants to, but cannot, he is impotent. If he can, but does not want to, he is wicked. If, as they say, God can abolish evil, and God really wants to do it, why is there evil in the world?

~ *Epicurus*

People only see what they are prepared to see.

~ *Ralph Waldo Emerson*

I ain't got no quarrel with the Vietcong ... No Vietcong ever called me nigger.

~ *Muhammad Ali, stripped of boxing title, sent to prison for refusing to serve during the Vietnam War*

If thou trusteth to the book called the Scriptures, thou trusteth to the rotten staff of fables and falsehood.

~ *Thomas Paine*

Our envy of others devours us most of all.

~ *Alexander Solzhenitsyn*

Lying is done with words and also with silence.

~ *Adrienne Rich*

If a man would follow, today, the teachings of the Old Testament, he would be a criminal. If he would follow strictly the teachings of the New, he would be insane.

~ *Robert G. Ingersoll*

I can envision a small cottage somewhere, with a lot of writing paper, and a dog, and a fireplace and maybe enough money to give myself some Irish coffee now and then and entertain my two friends.

~ *Richard Van de Geer, letter, 1975, last American to die in Vietnam War, Time, 1985*

If you are required to kill someone today, on the promise of a political leader that someone else shall live in peace tomorrow, believe me, you are not only a double murderer, you are a suicide, too.

~ *Katherine Anne Porter*

I spent thirty-three years in the marines, most of my time being a high-class muscle man for big business, for Wall Street and the bankers. In short, I was a racketeer for capitalism.

~ *General Smedley Butler, Marine Commandant*

Do not take life too seriously; you will never get out if it alive.

~ *Elbert Hubbard*

Delay is preferable to error.

~ *Thomas Jefferson*

If the critics unanimously take exception to one particular scene it is advisable to move that scene to a more conspicuous place in the program.

~ *Noel Coward*

I have seldom met an intelligent person whose views were not narrowed and distorted by religion.

~ *James Buchanan*

The music field was the first to break down racial barriers, because in order to play together, you have to love the people you are playing with, and if you have any racial inhibitions, you wouldn't be able to do that.

~ *Oscar Peterson*

The man who accumulates, whether money or knowledge, can never be free.

~ *J. Krishnamurthi*

Never cut what you can untie.

~ *Joseph Houbert*

The theory of a free press is that truth will emerge from free discussion, not that it will be presented perfectly and instantly in any one account.

~ *Walter Lippmann*

There is a tragic clash between truth and the world. Pure undistorted truth burns up the world.

~ *Nikolay Berdyayev*

Just drive down that road, until you get blown up.

~ *General George Patton, reconnaissance troops*

If I could find a way to get [Saddam Hussein] out of there, even putting a contract out on him, ... ahh ... if the CIA still did that sort of thing, . . . ahh . . . assuming it ever did . . . . I would be for it.

~ *Richard Nixon*

God give me strength to face a fact though it slay me.

~ *Thomas Huxley*

If a politician tells you he's going to make a realistic decision, you immediately understand that he's resolved to do something bad.

~ *Mary McCarthy*

I never advocated war except as a means of peace.

~ *Ulysses S. Grant*

If you pray for rain long enough, it eventually does fall. If you pray for floodwaters to abate, they eventually do. The same happens in the absence of prayers.

~ *Steve Allen*

Which is it, is man one of God's blu
of man's?

~ *Nietzsche*

What we have done for ourselves alone die ,
what we have done for others and the world ains
and is immortal.

~ *Albert Pike*

Humanity without religion is like a serial killer without a chainsaw.

~ *Unknown*

I hit him to get his attention. I shot him to calm him down. I killed him to reason with him.

~ *Henry Rollins*

Turn over the pages of history and read the damning record of the church's opposition to every advance in every field of science.

~ *Upton Sinclair*

Men are not punished for their sins, but by them.

~ *Elbert G Hubbard*

We have the wolf by the ears; and we can neither hold him, nor safely let him go. Justice is in one scale, and self-preservation in the other.

~ *Thomas Jefferson*

The same people that wrote the bible thought the world was flat.

~ *Unknown*

Spiritual maturity is a lifelong process of replacing lies with truth.

~ *Kurt Bruner*

e beauty perishes, but not in art.

~ *Leonardo da Vinci*

It is a government of the people by the people for the people no longer; it is a government of corporations by corporations for corporations.

~ *Rutherford B. Hayes*

Justice is too good for some people and not good enough for the rest.

~ *Norman Douglas*

Intellectuals solve problems; geniuses prevent them.

~ *Albert Einstein*

Mankind has been created for the sake of one another. Either instruct them, therefore, or endure them.

~ *Tacitus*

Lee Harvey Oswald, shooting from the top floor of the Book Depository was able to take three shots from an old misaligned Italian bolt action rifle. From a distance of over two-hundred and fifty-eight feet and shooting at a moving target he was able to score two hits including a headshot. Now does anybody know where he learned to shoot like this? In the Marine Corps ladies!

~ *Full Metal Jacket*

I was under medication when I made the decision to burn the tapes.

~ *Richard Nixon*

In computer science, we stand on each other's feet.

~ *Brian K. Reid*

But it does move.

~ *Galileo Galilei, after his trial*

Now, my good man, this is no time for making enemies.
~ *Voltaire, deathbed, when asked to renounce Satan*

We can't buy more time, cause time won't accept our money.
~ *Bad Religion*

The world in which we live can be understood as a result of muddle and accident; but if it is the outcome of deliberate purpose, the purpose must have been that of a fiend. For my part, I find accident a less painful and more plausible hypothesis.
~ *Bertrand Russell*

The criteria are fairly clear: a rogue state is not simply a criminal state, but one that defies the orders of the powerful who are, of course, exempt.
~ *Noam Chomsky*

Democracy is the art and science of running the circus from the monkey-cage.
~ *H. L. Mencken*

All our lauded technological progress, our very civilization, is like the axe in the hand of the pathological criminal.
~ *Albert Einstein*

When I was a boy I was told that anybody could become President. Now I'm beginning to believe it.
~ *Clarence Darrow*

New opinions are always suspected, and usually opposed, without any other reason but because they are not already common.
~ *John Locke*

Nothing in excess.

~ *Inscription, temple of Apollo at Delphi*

To put the world in order, we must first put the nation in order; to put the nation in order, we must put the family in order; to put the family in order, we must cultivate our personal life; and to cultivate our personal life, we must first set our hearts right.

~ *Confucius*

I can't tell the difference between the Evening News and Hill Street Blues.

~ *Bono*

Acceptance without proof is the fundamental characteristic of Western religion, rejection without proof is the fundamental characteristic of Western science.

~ *Gary Zukav*

Thou should not become presumptuous through much treasure and wealth; for in the end it is necessary for thee to leave all.

~ *Zoroaster*

How can you make a revolution without executions?

~ *Nikolai Lenin on hearing that the death penalty had been abolished by the Soviet*

True and false are attributes of speech, not of things. And where speech is not, there is neither truth nor falsehood.

~ *Thomas Hobbes*

The supreme happiness in life is the conviction that we are loved.

~ *Victor Hugo*

Do you love your Creator? Love your fellow beings first.
~ *Prophet Muhammad*

The absent are always in the wrong.
~ *Philippe Néricault Destouches*

Aryan people believe that they can decide their destiny. All people can determine their destiny, but sometimes they cannot because big power, including nature, exists around us. It is the same for Aryan.
~ *Toki Udagawa Chiba*

Laws are silent in time of war.
~ *Cicero*

Always recognize that human individuals are ends, and do not use them as means to your end.
~ *Immanuel Kant*

There cannot be a crisis next week. My schedule is already full.
~ *Henry Kissinger*

I shall be an autocrat: that's my trade. And the good Lord will forgive me: that's his.
~ *Empress Catherine the Great*

They that approve a private opinion, call it opinion; but they that mislike it, heresy: and yet heresy signifies no more than private opinion.
~ *René Descartes*

Man was born free, and everywhere he is in chains.
~ *Rousseau*

Never go to sleep when your meat is on the fire.
~ *Pueblo*

Clarity is learned by being patient in the presence of chaos.

~ *Lao tzu*

The country is headed toward a single and splendid government of an aristocracy founded on banking institution and monied incorporations and if this tendency continues, it will be the end of freedom and democracy; the few will be ruling and riding over the plundered plowman and the beggar in the omenry.

~ *Thomas Jefferson*

A treatise upon human nature: It is not contrary to reason to prefer the destruction of the whole world to the scratching of my finger.

~ *David Hume*

You can't step twice into the same river.

~ *Heraclitus*

You should never wear your best trousers when you go out to fight for freedom and liberty.

~ *Henrik Ibsen*

It is neither wealth nor splendor, but tranquility and occupation that give happiness.

~ *Thomas Jefferson*

Is that which is holy loved by the gods because it is holy, or is it holy because it is loved by the gods?

~ *Plato*

All kings is mostly rapscallions.

~ *Mark Twain*

Necessity never made a good bargain.

~ *Ben Franklin*

You shall find out how salt is the taste of another man's bread, and how hard is the way up and down another man's stairs.

~ *Dante*

You'll never have a quiet world till you knock the patriotism out of the human race.

~ *George Bernard Shaw*

The only good Indian is a dead Indian.

~ *Philip Henry Sheridan*

Human history becomes more and more a race between education and catastrophe.

~ *H. G. Wells*

You're not to be so blind with patriotism that you can't face reality. Wrong is wrong, no matter who does it or says it.

~ *Malcolm X*

I would rather be tied to the soil as another man's serf, even a poor man's, who hadn't much to live on himself, than be King of all these the dead and destroyed.

~ *Homer*

My people and I have come to an agreement, which satisfies us both. They are to say what they please, and I am to do what I please.

~ *Jean-Jacques Rousseau*

A wise man knows one thing: that he knows nothing.

~ *Confucius*

Sometimes I go about in pity for myself and all the while a Great Wind is bearing me across the sky.

~ *Ojibwa Saying*

God is subtle but he is not malicious.
~ *Albert Einstein*

The real differences around the world today are not between Jews and Arabs; Protestants and Catholics; Muslims, Croats, and Serbs. The real differences are between those who embrace peace and those who would destroy it; between those who look to the future and those who cling to the past; between those who open their arms and those who are determined to clench their fists.
~ *William J. Clinton*

The Pope!?! How many divisions has he got?
~ *Joseph Stalin*

I love you when you bow in your mosque, kneel in your temple, pray in your church; for you and I are sons of one religion and it is the spirit.
~ *Kahlil Gibran*

You manifestly wrong even the poorest ploughman, if you demand not his free consent.
~ *Charles I*

Never make a defense or apology before you be accused.
~ *Charles I*

This is very true; for my words are my own, and my actions are my ministers.
~ *Charles II*

Science has done more for the development of western civilization in one hundred years than Christianity did in eighteen hundred years.
~ *Jeff Burroughs*

Politics is war without bloodshed while war is politics with bloodshed.

~ *Mao Tse Tung*

Whatever is begun in anger ends in shame.

~ *Ben Franklin*

Tolerance is the ability to look beyond your ignorance; a sure sign of maturation.

~ *John Mann*

To show the fly the way out of the fly-bottle.

~ *Ludwig Wittgenstein, when asked, what is your aim in philosophy?*

The great nations have always acted like gangsters, and the small nations like prostitutes.

~ *Stanley Kubrick*

Facts do not cease to exist because they are ignored.

~ *Aldous Huxley*

When you call yourself an Indian or a Muslim or a Christian or a European, or anything else, you are being violent. Do you see why it is violent? It is because you are separating yourself from the rest of mankind. When you separate yourself by belief, by nationality, by tradition, it breeds violence. So a man who is seeking to understand violence does not belong to any country, to any religion, to any political party or partial system; he is concerned with the total understanding of mankind.

~ *J. Krishnamurthi*

It is my conviction that killing under the cloak of war is nothing but an act of murder.

~ *Albert Einstein*

It's a dangerous thing to think we know everything.
~ *Jack Kuehler*

Poverty is the worst form of violence.
~ *Mohandas Gandhi*

Beware of the fury of a patient man.
~ *John Dryden*

Well done is better than well said.
~ *Ben Franklin*

Trust in Allah, but tie your camel.
~ *Old Muslim Proverb*

I'm so sick of arming the world, then sending troops over to destroy the fucking arms; you know what I mean? We keep arming these little countries, then we go and blow the shit out of them. We're like the bullies of the world, y'know. We're like Jack Palance in the movie Shane, throwing the pistol at the sheepherder's feet.
'Pick it up.'
'I don't wanna pick it up, mister, you'll shoot me.'
'Pick up the gun.'
'Mister, I don't want no trouble, I just came downtown here to get some hard rock candy for my kids, some gingham for my wife. I don't even know what gingham is, but she goes through about ten rolls a week of that stuff. I ain't looking for no trouble, Mister.'
'Pick up the gun.'
The sheepherder picks up the gun, three shots ring out.
'You all saw him, he had a gun.'
~ *Bill Hicks*

Sometimes a scream is better than a thesis.
~ *Ralph Waldo Emerson*

As we look deeply within, we understand our perfect balance. There is no fear of the cycle of birth, life and death. For when you stand in the present moment, you are timeless.

~ *Rodney Yee*

There are very few monsters who warrant the fear we have of them.

~ *Andre Gide*

The whole aim of practical politics is to keep the populace alarmed and hence clamorous to be led to safety; by menacing it with an endless series of hobgoblins, all of them imaginary.

~ *H. L. Mencken*

The belief in the possibility of a short decisive war appears to be one of the most ancient and dangerous of human illusions.

~ *Robert Lynd*

Such prosperity as we have known it up to the present is the consequence of rapidly spending the planet's irreplaceable capital.

~ *Aldous Huxley*

I admire Confucius. He was the first man who did not receive a divine inspiration.

~ *Voltaire*

Always remember others may hate you but those who hate you don't win unless you hate them. And then you destroy yourself.

~ *Richard Nixon*

The more we sweat in peace the less we bleed in war.

~ *Vijaya Lakshmi Pandit*

So act that your principle of action might safely be made a law for the whole world.

~ *Immanuel Kant*

All difficult things have their origin in that which is easy, and great things in that which is small.

~ *Lao tzu*

I think people want peace so much that one of these days governments had better get out of the way and let them have it.

~ *Dwight D. Eisenhower*

Under democracy one party always devotes its chief energies to trying to prove that the other party is unfit to rule, and both commonly succeed, and are right.

~ *H. L. Mencken*

Whoever controls the media, the images, controls the culture.

~ *Allen Ginsberg*

The differences between the conservative and the radical seem to spring mainly from their attitude toward the future. Fear of the future causes us to lean against and cling to the present, while faith in the future renders us receptive to change.

~ *Eric Hoffer*

If a due participation of office is a matter of right, how are vacancies to be obtained? Those by death are few; by resignation none.

~ *Thomas Jefferson*

The moment you cheat for the sake of beauty, you know you are an artist.

~ *Max Jacob*

War is a ritual, a deadly ritual, not the result of aggressive self-assertion, but of self-transcending identification. Without loyalty to tribe, church, flag or ideal, there would be no wars.

~ *Arthur Koestler*

Those who do not feel pain, seldom think that it is felt.

~ *Samuel Johnson*

When you are right you cannot be too radical; when you are wrong you cannot be too conservative.

~ *Martin Luther King, Jr.*

Hatred does not cease by hatred, but only by love; this is the eternal rule.

~ *Buddha*

Patriotism is often an arbitrary veneration of real estate above principles.

~ *George Jean Nathan*

Executive ability is deciding quickly and getting somebody else to do the work.

~ *John Pollard*

Politics is a pendulum whose swings between anarchy and tyranny are fueled by perpetually rejuvenated illusions.

~ *Albert Einstein*

He who is of a calm and happy nature will hardly feel the pressure of age, but to him who is of an opposite disposition; youth and age are equally a burden.

~ *Plato*

Listen or your tongue will keep you deaf.

~ *Native American saying*

The trouble with the world is not that people know too little, but that they know so many things that ain't so.

~ *Mark Twain*

One-tenth of the folks run the world. One-tenth watch them run it, and the other eighty percent don't know what the hell's going on.

~ *Jake Simmons*

Civil disobedience, that's not our problem. Our problem is that people are obedient all over the world in the face of poverty and starvation and stupidity, and war, and cruelty. Our problem is that people are obedient while the jails are full of petty thieves, and all the while the grand thieves are running the country. That's our problem.

~ *Howard Zinn*

Conscience is, in most men, an anticipation of the opinion of others.

~ *Sir Henry Taylor*

If a man does not know to what port he is steering, no wind is favorable to him.

~ *Seneca*

War is one of the scourges with which it has pleased God to afflict men.

~ *Cardinal Richelieu*

True artists are almost the only men who do their work with pleasure.

~ *Auguste Rodin*

Things that are done out of self-interest produce a lot of resentment.

~ *Confucius*

Yesterday is gone. Tomorrow has not yet come. We have only today. Let us begin.

~ *Mother Teresa*

Truly to moderate your mind and speech when you are angry, or else to hold your peace, betokens no ordinary nature.

~ *Cicero*

Altogether national hatred is something peculiar. You will always find it strongest and most violent where there is the lowest degree of culture.

~ *Johann Wolfgang von Goethe*

Equality may perhaps be a right, but no power on earth can ever turn it into a fact.

~ *Honore de Balzac*

Never mistake knowledge for wisdom. One helps you make a living; the other helps you make a life.

~ *Sandara Carey*

All those that believe in telekinesis, raise my hand.

~ *Steven Wright*

The whole history of civilization is strewn with creeds and institutions which were invaluable at first, and deadly afterwards.

~ *Walter Bagehot*

Puritanism is the haunting fear that someone, somewhere, may be happy.

~ *H. L. Mencken*

It is a kingly action; believe me, to come to help of those who are fallen.

~ *Ovid*

When a stupid man is doing something he is ashamed of, he always declares that it is his duty.
~ *George Bernard Shaw*

The old believe everything: the middle-aged suspect everything: the young know everything.
~ *Oscar Wilde*

America did not invent human rights. In a very real sense, human rights invented America.
~ *Jimmy Carter*

Free curiosity is of more value than harsh discipline.
~ *Saint Augustine*

Civilization degrades the many to exalt the few.
~ *Bronson Alcott*

An empty stomach is not a good political advisor.
~ *Albert Einstein*

I'm ineffably tired of pro-war ideologues moaning about how the anti-war folk are just 'complaining' without 'offering solutions' to global dilemmas. Peace doesn't need a freekin moral, ethical, economical, or political qualification; war does. Peace doesn't ravage, plunder, rape, or kill; war does. Peace does not need justification, war does.
~ <|*OnAir*|>

Two things a man should never be angry at: what he can help, and what he cannot help.
~ *Thomas Fuller*

The first and simplest emotion which we discover in the human mind is curiosity.
~ *Edmond Burke*

Usually when people are sad, they don't do anything. They just cry over their condition. But when they get angry, they bring about a change.

~ *Malcolm X*

Everything I did in my life that was worthwhile I caught hell for.

~ *Earl Warren*

Nothing endures but personal qualities.

~ *Walt Whitman*

They always say time changes things, but you actually have to change them yourself.

~ *Andy Warhol*

It is by its promise of an occult sense of power that evil often attracts the weak.

~ *Eric Hoffer*

Noble people cherish virtue; petty people cherish property. Noble people hope for justice; petty people hope for favors.

~ *Confucius*

Thirty spokes converge upon a single hub; it is on the hole in the center that the cart hinges. We make a vessel from a lump of clay; it is the empty space within the vessel that makes it useful. We make doors and windows for a room; but it is these empty spaces that make the room livable. Thus, while the tangible has its uses, it is the intangible that makes it useful.

~ *Lao tzu*

What difference is there between us, save a restless dream that follows my soul but fears to come near you?

~ *Kahlil Gibran*

Not everything that can be counted counts and not everything that counts can be counted.
~ *Albert Einstein*

One must learn from the bite of the fire to leave it alone.
~ *Dakota*

The strongest man in the world is he who stands most alone.
~ *Hendrik Ibsen*

Religion is the end of love and honesty, the beginning of confusion; faith is a colorful hope or fear, the origin of folly.
~ *Tao Te Ching*

Over breakfast coffee we read of 40,000 American dead in Vietnam. Instead of vomiting, we reach for the toast. Our morning rush through crowded streets is not to cry murder but to hit that trough before somebody else gobbles our share.
~ *Dalton Trumbo*

If pigs could vote, the man with the slop bucket would be elected swineherd every time, no matter how much slaughtering he did on the side.
~ *Orson Scott Card*

It is good to die before one has done anything deserving death.
~ *Ananandrides*

Patriotism is your conviction that this country is superior to all other countries because you were born in it.
~ *George Bernard Shaw*

Why do we kill people who are killing people to show that killing people is wrong?

~ *Holly Near*

The tyranny of a multitude is a multiplied tyranny.

~ *Edmond Burke*

Conceit is incompatible with understanding.

~ *Leo Tolstoy*

A Native American elder once described his own inner struggles in this manner: 'Inside of me there are two dogs. One of the dogs is mean and evil. The other dog is good. The mean dog fights the good dog all the time.' When asked which dog wins, he reflected for a moment and replied, 'The one I feed the most.'

If you give me six lines written by the hand of the most honest of men, I will find something in them which will hang him.

~ *Cardinal Richelieu*

Every decision is liberating, even if it leads to disaster. Otherwise, why do so many people walk upright and with open eyes into their misfortune?

~ *Elias Canetti*

The public have an insatiable curiosity to know everything, except what is worth knowing.

~ *Oscar Wilde*

The world is weary of statesmen whom democracy has degraded into politicians.

~ *Benjamin Disraeli*

Only a fool tests the depth of the water with both feet.

~ *African proverb*

Democracy is the recurrent suspicion that more than half of the people are right more than half of the time.

~ *Elwyn B. White*

Every major horror of history was committed in the name of an altruistic motive.

~ *Ayn Rand*

To be independent is the business of a few only; it is the privilege of the strong.

~ *Nietzsche*

One enemy can do more hurt than ten friends can do good.

~ *Jonathan Swift*

Where thou art obliged to speak, be sure to speak the truth; for equivocation is half way to lying, as lying, the whole way to hell.

~ *William Penn*

The more I study religions the more I am convinced that man never worshipped anything but himself.

~ *Sir R. F. Burton*

Do what you can, with what you have, where you are.

~ *Theodore Roosevelt*

Truth, purity and unselfishness, wherever these three are present, there is no power below or above the sun to crush the possessor thereof. Equipped with these one individual is able to face the universe in opposition.

~ *Swamy Vivekananda*

We are ensnared by the wisdom of the serpent; we are set free by the foolishness of God.

~ *Saint Augustine*

We live in our desires rather than in our achievements.
~ *George Moore*

Reality is a mere illusion, albeit a persistent one.
~ *Albert Einstein*

A scholar who cherishes the love of comfort is not fit to be deemed a scholar.
~ *Lao Tsu*

Did I follow Truth wherever she led, and stand against the whole world for a cause, and uphold the weak against the strong? If I did, I would be remembered among men...
~ *Edgar Lee Masters*

The opposite of a correct statement is a false statement. The opposite of a profound truth may well be another profound truth.
~ *Niels Bohr*

I respect faith, but doubt is what gets you an education.
~ *Wilson Mizner*

X-rays will prove to be a hoax.
~ *Lord Kelvin*

If you seek truth, you will not seek to gain a victory by every possible means; and when you have found truth, you need not fear being defeated.
~ *Epictetus*

The enormous gap between what US leaders do in the world and what Americans think their leaders are doing is one of the great propaganda accomplishments of the dominant political mythology.
~ *Michael Parenti*

Wherever there is great property, there is great inequality, for one very rich man; there must be at least five hundred poor.

~ *Adam Smith*

The progress of the rivers to the ocean is not so rapid as that of man to error.

~ *Voltaire*

The sad truth is that most evil is done by people who never make up their minds to be either good or evil.

~ *Hannah Arendt*

When a government lasts a long while, it deteriorates by insensible degrees. Republics end through luxury, monarchies through poverty.

~ *Montesquieu*

The cardinal doctrine of a fanatic's creed is that his enemies are the enemies of God.

~ *Andrew Dickson White*

Believing ourselves to be possessors of absolute truth degrades us: we regard every person whose way of thinking is different from ours as a monster and a threat and by so doing turn our own selves into monsters and threats to our fellows.

~ *Octavio Paz*

Faith is much better than belief. Belief is when someone else does the thinking.

~ *Richard Buckminster Fuller*

I slept with Faith, and woke to find myself in bed with a corpse. I danced all night with Doubt, and found her a virgin in the morning.

~ *Aleister Crowley*

Skepticism is the first step on the road to philosophy.
~ *Denis Diderot*

The more a man dreams, the less he believes.
~ *H. L. Mencken*

His Lordship may compel us to be equal upstairs, but there will never be equality in the servants' hall.
~ *James M. Barrie*

Freedom is not something that anybody can be given, freedom is something people take.
~ *James Baldwin*

The public is wonderfully tolerant. It forgives everything except genius.
~ *Oscar Wilde*

If you don't believe drugs have done good things for us, then go home and burn all your records, all your tapes, and all your CDs, because every one of those artists who have made brilliant music and enhanced your lives were RrrrrrrrrrrrrrrrrEAL fucking high on drugs. The Beatles were so fucking high they let Ringo sing a few songs.
~ *Bill Hicks*

The defects of great men are consolation of dunces.
~ *Isaac D'Israeli*

Christianity persecuted, tortured, and burned. Like a hound, it tracked the very scent of heresy. It kindled wars, and nursed furious hatreds and ambitions. Man, far from being freed from his natural passions, was plunged into artificial ones quite as violent and much more disappointing.
~ *George Santayana*

A wicked man is his own hell.
~ *Thomas Fuller*

Custom is the principal magistrate of man's life.
~ *Francis Bacon*

Man is the religious animal. He is the only religious animal. He is the only animal that has the True Religion, several of them. He is the only animal that loves his neighbor as himself and cuts his throat, if his theology isn't straight. He has made a graveyard of the globe in trying his honest best to smooth his brother's path to happiness and heaven.
~ *Mark Twain*

Those who forgive most shall be most forgiven.
~ *Philip James Bailey*

Often the fear of one evil leads us into worse.
~ *Nicolas Boileau*

Every man is his own greatest enemy, and as it were his own executioner.
~ *Sir Thomas Browne*

Fear, like pain, looks and sounds worse than it feels.
~ *Rebecca West*

The most unfree souls go west and shout of freedom. Men are freest when they are most unconscious of freedom. The shout is a rattling of chains.
~ *David H. Lawrence*

Society in every state is a blessing, but government, even in its best stage, is but a necessary evil; in its worst stage, an intolerable one.
~ *Thomas Paine*

The supreme art of war is to subdue the enemy without fighting.

~ *Sun tzu*

No one can be perfectly free till all are free.

~ *Herbert Spencer*

A foolish consistency is the hobgoblin of little minds, adored by little statesmen and philosophers and divines.

~ *Ralph Waldo Emerson*

Know all and you will pardon all.

~ *Thomas à Kempis*

The greatest pleasure I know is to do a good action by stealth, and to have it found out by accident.

~ *Charles Lamb*

Habit is a cable; we weave a thread of it every day, and at last we cannot break it.

~ *Horace Mann*

He who imitates what is evil always goes beyond the example that is set; on the contrary, he who imitates what is good always falls short.

~ *Francesco Guicciardini*

It is easier to lead men to combat, stirring up their passion, than to restrain them and direct them toward the patient labors of peace.

~ *Andre Gide*

Truthful words are not beautiful; beautiful words are not truthful. Good words are not persuasive; persuasive words are not good.

~ *Lao tzu*

Distrust all in whom the impulse to punish is powerful.
~ *Nietzsche*

Prohibition goes beyond reason in that it attempts to control a man's appetite through legislation. A prohibition law strikes a blow at the very principles this country was founded upon.
~ *Abraham Lincoln*

They that die by famine die by inches.
~ *Matthew Henry*

There is no sport in hate when all the rage is on one side.
~ *Percy B. Shelley*

There is always a certain meanness in the argument of conservatism, joined with a certain superiority in its fact.
~ *Ralph Waldo Emerson*

Force always attracts men of low morality, and I believe it to be an invariable rule that tyrants of genius are succeeded by scoundrels.
~ *Albert Einstein*

I searched through rebellion, drugs, diets, mysticism, religions, intellectualism and much more, only to begin to find that truth is basically simple; and feels good, clean and right.
~ *Chick Corea*

All natural institutions of churches, whether Jewish, Christian, or Turkish, appear to me no other than human inventions, set up to terrify and enslave mankind, and monopolize power and profit.
~ *Thomas Paine*

It is not a matter of wishing success to the victim of aggression, but of sharing his fate, one must accompany him to his death or to victory.

~ *Ernesto 'Che' Guevara*

History is the sum total of things that could have been avoided.

~ *Konrad Adenauer*

Make yourself an honest man, and then you may be sure that there is one rascal less in the world.

~ *Thomas Carlyle*

It is as hard for the good to suspect evil, as it is for the bad to suspect good.

~ *Cecero*

Oh, how bitter a thing is to look through another man's eye.

~ *William Shakespeare*

In law a man is guilty when he violates the rights of another. In ethics he is guilty if he only thinks of doing so.

~ *Immanuel Kant*

Goodness is a special kind of truth and beauty. It is truth and beauty in human behavior.

~ *Harry A. Overstreet*

The majority cares little for ideals and integrity. What it craves is display.

~ *Emma Goldman*

My humble friend, we know not how to live this life which is so short yet seek one that never ends.

~ *Anatole France*

I am sufficiently proud of my knowing something to be modest about my not knowing everything.

~ *Vladimir Nabokov*

Heaven gives long life to the just and the intelligent.

~ *Confucius*

Society cares about the individual only in so far as he is profitable.

~ *Simone de Beauvoir*

Except as its clown and jester, society does not encourage individuality, and the State abhors it.

~ *Bernard Berenson*

I never think of the future, it will come soon enough.

~ *Albert Einstein*

To the ignorant, even the words of the wise seem foolishness.

~ *Euripides*

I have three precious things which I hold fast and prize. The first is gentleness; the second is frugality; the third is humility, which keeps me from putting myself before others. Be gentle and you can be bold; be frugal and you can be liberal; avoid putting yourself before others and you can become a leader among men.

~ *Lao tzu*

Every fire is the same size when it starts.

~ *Seneca*

When you philosophically oppose an entire power elite, you cannot help but sound like a conspiracy theorist. Social power is by nature a conspiracy.

~ *Tom N*

Love is only the dirty trick played on us to achieve continuation of the species.

~ *William Somerset Maugham*

I assure you, I had rather excel others in the knowledge of what is excellent, than in the extent of my power and dominion.

~ *Alexander the Great*

You must ask your neighbor if you shall live in peace.

~ *John Clark*

Education ... has produced a vast population able to read but unable to distinguish what is worth reading.

~ *George M. Trevelyan*

It is true that liberty, so precious, must be rationed.

~ *Nikolai Lenin*

One man's magic is another man's engineering. Supernatural is a null word.

~ *Robert Heinlein*

Religion, comprises a system of wishful illusions together with a disavowal of reality, such as we find in an isolated form nowhere else but in amentia, in a state of blissful hallucinatory confusion.

~ *Sigmund Freud*

It would now be technically possible to unify the world, abolish war and poverty altogether, if men desired their own happiness more than the misery of their enemies.

~ *Bertrand Russel*

Laughter is not a bad beginning for friendship, and it is the best ending for one.

~ *Oscar Wilde*

Most men lead lives of quiet desperation and go to the grave with the song still in them.

~ *Henry David Thoreau*

Art is dangerous. It is one of the attractions: when it ceases to be dangerous, you don't want it.

~ *Duke Ellington*

I refuse to be labeled immoral merely because I am godless.

~ *Peter Walker*

Suppose you were an idiot, and suppose you were a member of congress; but I repeat myself.

~ *Mark Twain*

Real pain can alone cure us of imaginary ills.

~ *Jonathan Edwards*

Life is like a game of cards. The hand that is dealt you represents determinism; the way you play it is free will.

~ *Jawaharlal Nehru*

In the arts of life man invents nothing; but in the arts of death he outdoes Nature herself, and produces by chemistry and machinery all the slaughter of plague, pestilence, and famine.

~ *George Bernard Shaw*

How long would authority ... exist, if not for the willingness of the mass to become soldiers, policemen, jailers, and hangmen.

~ *Emma Goldman*

Know thy enemy and know thy self and you will win a hundred battles.

~ *Sun tzu*

How good bad music and bad reasons sound when we march against an enemy!

~ *Nietzsche*

To perceive is to suffer.

~ *Aristotle*

A lot of Christians wear crosses around their necks. Do you think when Jesus comes back he ever wants to see a fuckin' cross? It's kind of like going up to Jackie Onassis with a rifle pendant on.

~ *Bill Hicks*

In nothing do men more nearly approach the gods than in doing good to their fellow men.

~ *Cicero*

Science bestowed immense new powers on man and at the same time creates conditions, which were largely beyond his comprehension and still more beyond his control.

~ *Winston Churchill*

To pity distress is but human: to relieve it is Godlike.

~ *Horace Mann*

A large part of altruism, even when it is perfectly honest, is grounded upon the fact that it is uncomfortable to have unhappy people about one.

~ *H. L. Mencken*

Children begin by loving their parents; as they grow older they judge them; sometimes they forgive them.

~ *Oscar Wilde*

The hands that help are holier than the lips that pray.

~ *Robert G. Ingersoll*

An insincere and evil friend is more to be feared than a wild beast; a wild beast may wound your body, but an evil friend will wound your mind.

~ *Buddha*

The optimist proclaims that we live in the best of all possible worlds; and the pessimist fears this is true.

~ *James Branch Cabell*

Peace is only possible if men cease to place their happiness in the possession of things which cannot be shared.

~ *Julien Benda*

Every blade of grass has an angel that bends over it and whispers, 'Grow! Grow!'

~ *The Talmud*

The first panacea for a mismanaged nation is inflation of the currency; the second is war. Both bring a temporary prosperity; both bring a permanent ruin. But both are the refuge of political and economic opportunists.

~ *Ernest Hemingway*

The politician is an acrobat. He keeps his balance by saying the opposite of what he does.

~ *Maurice Barrès*

Oh, God, if I were sure to die tonight I would repent at once. It is the commonest prayer in all languages.

~ *James M. Barrie*

The truth is that there is nothing noble in being superior to somebody else. The only real nobility is in being superior to your former self.

~ *Whitney Young*

The fewer desires, the more peace.
~ *Thomas Wilson*

It may be necessary temporarily to accept a lesser evil, but one must never label a necessary evil as good.
~ *Margaret Mead*

Humankind cannot stand very much reality.
~ *T. S. Eliot*

Silence is one of the hardest arguments to refute.
~ *Josh Billings*

If stupidity got us into this mess, then why can't it get us out?
~ *Will Rogers*

Man who stand on hill with mouth open will wait long time for roast duck to drop in.
~ *Confucius*

My first wish is to see this plague of mankind, war, banished from the earth.
~ *George Washington*

Never forget that everything Hitler did in Germany was legal.
~ *Martin Luther King, Jr.*

Nothing gives one person so much advantage over another as to remain always cool and unruffled under all circumstances.
~ *Thomas Jefferson*

Every day people are straying away from the church and going back to God.
~ *Lenny Bruce*

In order to learn, one must change one's mind.
~ *Orson Scott Card*

Patriotism is the virtue of the vicious.
~ *Oscar Wilde*

Beware my lord of jealousy; it is the green-eyed monster that doth mock the meat it feeds on.
~ *William Shakespeare*

You can't wake a person who is pretending to be asleep.
~ *Native Proverb*

He will always be a slave, who does not know how to live upon a little.
~ *Horace*

Every anarchist is a baffled dictator.
~ *Benito Mussolini*

Do not do an immoral thing for moral reasons.
~ *Thomas Hardy*

He who slings mud, usually loses ground.
~ *Adlai Stevenson*

Physics is not a religion. If it were, we'd have a much easier time raising money.
~ *Leon Lederman*

I have often regretted my speech, never my silence.
~ *Xenocrates*

Prayer is always answered; it's just sometimes you don't like the answer.
~ *<deacon^>*

Never does nature say one thing and wisdom another.
~ *Juvenal*

He who will not reason is a bigot; he who cannot is a fool; and he who dares not is a slave.
~ *William Drummond*

Conservatives are not necessarily stupid, but most stupid people are conservatives.
~ *John Stuart Mill*

Taste and opinion cannot replace intelligence and knowledge.
~ *Man Ray*

True security can only be found in a maximum security prison Isolation cell, and even there, there is the imminent threat of release.
~ *Timothy Leary*

We have always known that heedless self-interest was bad morals; we know now that it is bad economics.
~ *Franklin D. Roosevelt*

The foolish and dead alone never change their opinion.
~ *James Russel Lowell*

War is the child of pride, and pride the daughter of riches.
~ *Jonathan Swift*

One cannot have the vision of God as long as one has these three: shame, hatred and fear.
~ *Sri Ramakrishna*

The quickest way of ending a war is to lose it.
~ *George Orwell*

The Tao doesn't take sides; it gives birth to both good and evil. The Master doesn't take sides; she welcomes both saints and sinners.

~ *Tao Te Ching*

Nothing in all the world is more dangerous than sincere ignorance and conscientious stupidity.

~ *Martin Luther King, Jr.*

Regret not that which is past; and trust not to thine own righteousness.

~ *Saint Anthony*

War is an instrument entirely insufficient toward redressing wrong; and multiplies, instead of indemnifying losses.

~ *Thomas Jefferson*

Truth always lags behind, limping along on the arm of Time.

~ *Baltasar Gracián*

Nothing unites the English like war. Nothing divides them like Picasso.

~ *Hugh Mills*

If there were only one single truth, it would not be possible to paint a hundred pictures of the same subject.

~ *Pablo Picasso*

A thing is not necessarily true because a man dies for it.

~ *Oscar Wilde*

...as hollow as the o in god...

~ *Marilyn Manson*

War: first, one hopes to win; then one expects the enemy to lose; then, one is satisfied that he too is suffering; in the end, one is surprised that everyone has lost.

~ *Karl Kraus*

I offer my opponents a bargain: if they will stop telling falsehoods about us, I will stop telling the truth about them.

~ *Adlai Stevenson*

A man who says he knows is already dead. But the man who thinks, I don't know, who is discovering, finding out, who is not seeking an end, not thinking in terms of arriving or becoming, such a man is living, and that living is truth.

~ *J. Krishnamurthi*

It may be that our role on this planet is not to worship God, but to create him.

~ *Arthur C. Clarke*

It is better to be generous than just. It is sometimes better to sympathize instead of trying to understand.

~ *Pierre Lecompte de Nouy*

To me, it seems a dreadful indignity to have a soul controlled by geography.

~ *George Santayana*

Learn from yesterday, live for today, hope for tomorrow. The important thing is to not stop questioning.

~ *Albert Einstein*

The more you own, the more it owns you.

~ *Henry Rollins*

Money often costs too much.

~ *Ralph Waldo Emerson*

It is hard, I submit, to loathe bloodshed, including war, more than I do, but it is still harder to exceed my loathing of the very nature of totalitarian states in which massacre is only an administrative detail.

~ *Vladimir Nabokov*

I have examined all of the known superstitions of the world and I do not find in our superstitions of Christianity one redeeming feature. They are all founded on fables and mythology. Christianity has made one-half the world fools and the other half hypocrites.

~ *Thomas Jefferson*

Nothing is more surprising than the easiness with which the many are governed by the few.

~ *David Hume*

And the little screaming fact that sounds through all history: repression works only to strengthen and knit the repressed.

~ *John Steinbeck*

So long as mankind shall continue to lavish more praise upon its destroyers than upon its benefactors, war shall remain the chief pursuit of ambitious minds.

~ *Edward Gibbon*

You shall judge a man by his foes as well as by his friends.

~ *Joseph Conrad*

We are condemned to kill time: thus we die bit by bit.

~ *Octavio Paz*

Do not seek to follow in the footsteps of the wise. Seek what they sought.

~ *Basho*

When a man dies, they who survive him ask what property he has left behind: The angel who bends over the dying man asks what good deed he has sent before him.

~ *The Quran*

Morality is the best of all devices for leading mankind by the nose.

~ *Nietzsche*

It is the deed that teaches, not the name we give it. Murder and capital punishment are not opposites that cancel one another, but similars that breed their kind.

~ *George Bernard Shaw*

By trying we can easily learn to endure adversity; another man's, I mean.

~ *Mark Twain*

The superior man is firm in the right way, and not merely firm.

~ *Confucius*

When one eye is fixed upon your destination, there is only one eye left with which to see the way there.

~ *Matthew Wallace*

Give to every other human being every right you claim for yourself.

~ *Robert G. Ingersoll*

The truth is more important than the facts.

~ *Frank Lloyd Wright*

A tyrant is always stirring up some war or other, in order that the people may require a leader.

~ *Plato*

We don't receive wisdom; we must discover it for ourselves after a journey that no one can take for us or spare us.

~ *Marcel Proust*

The wicked leader is he who the people despise. The good leader is he who the people revere. The great leader is he who the people say, 'We did it ourselves.

~ *Lao tzu*

I have not failed. I've just found ten thousand ways that don't work.

~ *Thomas Edison*

Don't say you don't have enough time. You have exactly the same number of hours per day that were given to Helen Keller, Pasteur, Michelangelo, Mother Teresa, Leonardo da Vinci, Thomas Jefferson, and Albert Einstein.

~ *H. Jackson Brown*

Life is pleasant. Death is peaceful. It's the transition that's troublesome.

~ *Jimi Hendrix*

Twenty years from now you will be more disappointed by the things that you didn't do than by the ones you did do.

~ *Samuel Clemens*

Wise men talk because they have something to say; fools, because they have to say something.

~ *Plato*

Ignorance is always afraid of change.
~ *Jawaharlal Nehru*

Youth is a blunder; manhood a struggle; old age a regret.
~ *Benjamin Disraeli*

Before we blame, we should first see if we can excuse.
~ *G. C. Lichtenberg*

A journey of a thousand miles must begin with a single step.
~ *Lao Tsu*

Besides the noble art of getting things done, there is a nobler art of leaving things undone ...The wisdom of life consists in the elimination of nonessentials.
~ *Lin Yutang*

My final point about alcohol, about drugs, about pornography; what business is it of yours what I do, read, buy, see, fuck or take into my body as long as I don't harm another human being whilst on this planet? And for those of you having a little moral dilemma on how to answer this, I'll answer for you. None of your fucking business! Take that to the bank, cash it and take it on a vacation outta my fucking life.
~ *Bill Hicks*

Don't speak unless you can improve on the silence.
~ *Spanish proverb*

The foundation of morality should not be made dependent on myth nor tied to any authority lest doubt about the myth or about the legitimacy of the authority imperil the foundation of sound judgment and action.
~ *Albert Einstein*

The shit you have to put up with is the shit you chose to take.

~ *Unknown*

I would have made a good pope.

~ *Richard Nixon*

In politics, stupidity is not a handicap.

~ *Napoleon*

I dream that someday the United States will be on the side of the peasants in some civil war. I dream that we will be the ones who will help the poor overthrow the rich, who will talk about land reform and education and health facilities for everyone, and that when the Red Cross or Amnesty International comes to count the bodies and take the testimony of women raped, that our side won't be the heavies.

~ *Richard Cohen*

Throughout the world, on any given day, a man, woman or child is likely to be displaced, tortured, killed or disappeared, at the hands of governments or armed political groups. More often than not, the United States shares the blame.

~ *Amnesty International, in its annual report on U.S. Military aid and human rights, 1996*

The purpose of law is to prevent the strong from always having their way.

~ *Ovid*

Good men must die, but death cannot kill their names.

~ *Proverbs*

Pity the warrior that kills all his foe.

~ *Star Trek*

Time is a great teacher, but unfortunately it kills all its pupils.

~ *Hector Berlioz*

The foolish man seeks happiness in the distance; the wise grows it under his feet.

~ *James Oppenheim*

As a rule, what is out of sight disturbs men's minds more seriously than what they see.

~ *Julius Caesar*

Faith is belief without evidence in what is told by one who speaks without knowledge, of things without parallel.

~ *Ambrose Bierce*

My opinions may have changed, but not the fact that I am right.

~ *Ashleigh Brilliant*

The greater danger for most of us lies not in setting our aim too high and falling short; but in setting our aim too low, and achieving our mark.

~ *Michelangelo*

Before you choose a counselor, watch him with his neighbor's children.

~ *Lakota*

I look at life as a gift of God. Now that he wants it back I have no right to complain.

~ *Joyce Cary*

The only interesting answers are those which destroy the questions.

~ *Susan Sontag*

The world is divided into people who think they are right.

~ *Unknown*

When you see the Earth from space, you don't see any divisions of nation-states there. This may be the symbol of the new mythology to come; this is the country we will celebrate, and these are the people we are one with.

~ *Joseph Campbell*

A man who is afraid will do anything.

~ *Jawaharlal Nehru*

Heresy is a cradle; orthodoxy a coffin.

~ *Robert G. Ingersoll*

Any fool can criticize, condemn, and complain, and most fools do.

~ *Ben Franklin*

Peace begins with a smile.

~ *Mother Teresa*

From this day forward, I no longer shall tinker with the machinery of death. I feel morally and intellectually obligated simply to concede that the death penalty experiment has failed. It is virtually self-evident to me now that no combination of procedural rules or substantive regulations ever can save the death penalty from its inherent constitutional deficiencies.

~ *Former US Supreme Court Justice Harry Blackmun*

The greatest purveyor of violence on earth is my own government.

~ *Martin Luther King, Jr.*

Patriotism is the last refuge of a scoundrel.

~ *Samuel Johnson, English lexicographer, to which Ambrose Bierce replied: 'I beg to submit that it is the first.'*

History is the propaganda of the victors.

~ *Ernst Toller*

All war is a symptom of man's failure as a thinking animal.

~ *John Steinbeck*

If you are out to describe the truth, leave elegance to the tailor.

~ *Albert Einstein*

The death penalty is based on ability-to-pay.

~ *Unknown*

Peace has never come from dropping bombs. Real peace comes from enlightenment and educating people to behave more in a divine manner.

~ *Carlos Santana*

The desire of food is limited in every man by the narrow capacity of the human stomach; but the desire of the conveniences and ornaments of building, dress, equipage and household furniture, seems to have no limit or certain boundary.

~ *Adam Smith*

The bitterest tears shed over graves are for words left unsaid and deeds left undone.

~ *Harriet Beecher Stowe*

Mysteries are not necessarily miracles.

~ *Johann Wolfgang von Goethe*

Your eyes cannot see the truth when your imagination is out of focus.

~ *Mark Twain*

Capitalism is the astounding belief that the most wickedest of men will do the most wickedest of things for the greatest good of everyone.

~ *John Maynard Keynes*

Why are the people rebellious? Because the rulers interfere too much, therefore they are rebellious.

~ *Lao tzu*

While the word is yet unspoken, you are master of it; when once it is spoken, it is master of you.

~ *Arab proverb*

The enemy is anybody who's going to get you killed, no matter which side he is on.

~ *Joseph Heller*

It makes no difference as to the name of the God, since love is the real God of all in the world.

~ *Apache*

Christianity exceeds all other faiths in its power to deform and finally invert the mental process.

~ *Ida White*

The fascist state is the corporate state.

~ *Benito Mussolini*

God favors no group. Only religions do that.

~ *Bumper Sticker*

Each of us is confined to a world of our own making.

~ *Shawn Mikula*

On the outskirts of every agony sits some observant fellow who points.

~ *Virginia Woolf*

You can only protect your liberties in this world by protecting the other man's freedom. I can only be free if you are free.

~ *Clarence Darrow*

Mr. Clinton better watch out if he comes down here. He'd better have a bodyguard.

~ *Jessie Helms*

Wise men, though all laws were abolished, would lead the same lives.

~ *Aristophanes*

Democracy used to be a good thing, but now it has gotten into the wrong hands.

~ *Jessie Helms*

A Roman Catholic priest and theologian have called on their church to consider the possibility of evangelizing extraterrestrials, according to published reports. After two Swiss astronomers said they had discovered the first planet in a solar system similar to Earth's, Piero Coda, a theology professor in Rome, said any beings living on the planet would be in need of salvation.

~ *Associated Baptist Press article*

It is impossible to defeat an ignorant man in argument.

~ *William Gibbs McAdoo*

I do not feel obliged to believe that the same God who has endowed us with sense, reason, and intellect has intended us to forgo their use.

~ *Galileo Galilei*

The Christian resolution to find the world ugly and bad has made the world ugly and bad.

~ *Nietzsche*

There are no whole truths; all truths are half-truths. It is trying to treat them as whole truths that play the devil.

~ *Alfred North Whitehead*

April First is the day upon which we are reminded of what we are on the other three hundred sixty-four.

~ *Mark Twain*

A good warrior is not bellicose, a good fighter does not anger, a good conqueror does not contest his enemy, one who is good at using others puts himself below them.

~ *Lao tzu*

Against stupidity, the Gods themselves contend in vain.

~ *Friedrich von Schiller*

Censorship is the height of vanity.

~ *Martha Graham*

The multitude of books is a great evil. There is no limit to this fever for writing.

~ *Martin Luther*

If the doctor told me I had only six minutes to live, I'd type a little faster.

~ *Isaac Asimov*

If a person is to get to the meaning of life, he must learn to like the facts about himself, ugly as they may seem to his sentimental vanity, before he can learn the truth behind the facts. And the truth is never ugly.

~ *Eugene O'Neill*

It is forbidden to kill; therefore all murderers are punished unless they kill in large numbers and to the sound of trumpets.

~ *Voltaire*

The modern conservative is engaged in one man's oldest exercises in moral philosophy; that is the search for a superior moral justification for selfishness.

~ *John K. Galbraith*

No one has ever had an idea in a dress suit.

~ *Sir Frederick G. Banting*

Without doubt, machinery has greatly increased the number of well-to-do idlers.

~ *Karl Marx*

Without censorship, things can get terribly confused in the public mind.

~ *General William Westmoreland*

Until the infallibility of human judgment shall have been proved to me, I shall persist in demanding the abolition of the death penalty.

~ *Marquis de Lafayette*

Once you make a decision, the universe conspires to make it happen.

~ *Ralph Waldo Emerson*

A conservative is a man who is too cowardly to fight and too fat to run.

~ *Elbert Hubbard*

If you don't know where you're going, any road will get you there.

~ *Ancient Chinese Proverb*

When a diplomat says `yes' he means perhaps; when he says `perhaps' he means no; when he says `no' he is no diplomat.

~ *Unknown*

I expect to pass through this world but once. Any good therefore that I can do, or any kindness that I can show to any fellow creature, let me do it now. Let me not defer or neglect it, for I shall not pass this way again.

~ *William Penn*

Opportunities multiply as they are seized.

~ *Sun tzu*

We must be willing to let go of the life we have planned, so as to have the life that is waiting for us.

~ *Joseph Campbell*

Strange is our situation here upon Earth.

~ *Albert Einstein*

Since it is impossible to escape the result of our deeds let us practice good works.

~ *Buddha*

Guns make us powerful; butter will only make us fat.

~ *Nazi Hermann Goering*

When the president does it that means it is not illegal.

~ *Richard Nixon*

Being a good craftsman will in no way prevent you from becoming a genius.

~ *Renoir*

Nobody ever died of laughter.

~ *Max Beerbohm*

War is hell and all that, but it has a good deal to recommend it. It wipes out all the small nuisances of peacetime.

~ *Ian Hay*

We cannot change anything until we accept it. Condemnation does not liberate, it oppresses.

~ *C. G. Jung*

Patriotism is the willingness to kill and be killed for trivial reasons.

~ *Bertrand Russell*

See, in my lone of work you got to keep repeating things over and over again for the truth to sink in … to kind of catapult the propaganda.

~ *George W. Bush*

I must do something.

~ *Mother Teresa*

All propaganda must be so popular and on such an intellectual level, that even the most stupid of those toward whom it is directed will understand it ... Through clever and constant application of propaganda, people can be made to see paradise as hell, and also the other way around, to consider the most wretched sort of life as paradise.

~ *Adolf Hitler*

Real knowledge is to know the extent of one's ignorance.

~ *Confucius*

The real measure of your wealth is how much you'd be worth if you lost all your money.

~ *Unknown*

I hope I never get so old I get religious.
~ *Ingmar Bergman*

You can tell whether a man is clever by his answers. You can tell whether a man is wise by his questions.
~ *Mahfouz Naguib*

Never worry about theory as long as the machinery does what it's supposed to do.
~ *Robert Heinlein*

Faith may be defined briefly as an illogical belief in the occurrence of the improbable.
~ *H. L. Mencken*

The greatest thing in this world is not so much where we are, but in what direction we are moving.
~ *Oliver Wendell Holmes*

Nothing in life is as exhilarating as to be shot at without result.
~ *Winston Churchill*

It [the Bible] is full of interest. It has noble poetry in it; and some clever fables; and some blood-drenched history; and some good morals; and a wealth of obscenity; and upwards of a thousand lies.
~ *Mark Twain*

Heresy is what the minority believe; it is the name given by the powerful to the doctrines of the weak.
~ *Robert G. Ingersoll*

I can retain neither respect nor affection for government, which has been moving from wrong to wrong in order to defend its immorality.
~ *Mohandas Gandhi*

I am tired of fighting, our chiefs are killed...it is cold and we have no blankets. The little children are freezing to death...hear me, my chiefs, I am tired: my heart is sick and sad. From where the sun now stands...I will fight no more forever...

~ *Chief Joseph, before his tribe was slaughtered*

It takes twenty years or more of peace to make a man; it takes only twenty seconds of war to destroy him.

~ *Baudouin I, King of Belgium*

You know, doing what is right is easy. The problem is knowing what is right.

~ *Lyndon B. Johnson*

Science should be taught not in order to support religion and not in order to destroy religion. Science should be taught simply ignoring religion.

~ *Steven Weinberg*

Confucianism may be a civilization, but it is not a religion.

~ *G. K. Chesterton*

Life's a great big canvas; throw all the paint you can at it.

~ *Danny Kaye*

As far as the laws of mathematics refer to reality, they are not certain, and as far as they are certain, they do not refer to reality.

~ *Albert Einstein*

It is the weakness and danger of republics, that the vices as well as the virtues of the people are represented in their legislation.

~ *Helen Maria Hunt Jackson*

One's mind, once stretched by a new idea, never regains its original dimensions.

~ *Oliver Wendell Holmes*

In a time of universal deceit, telling the truth is a revolutionary act.

~ *George Orwell*

Think my friends! You adulate a stone as Vishnu but you cannot see God in a fellow man.

~ *Sankaracharya*

There are no shortcuts to any place worth going.

~ *Beverly Sills*

Anger is a sort of madness and the noblest causes have been damaged by advocates affected with temporary lunacy.

~ *Mohandas Gandhi*

The Constitution only gives people the right to pursue happiness. You have to catch it yourself.

~ *Ben Franklin*

The total absence of humor in the Bible is one of the most singular things in all literature.

~ *Alfred North Whitehead*

A fool always finds one still more foolish to admire him.

~ *Nicolas Boileau*

God enjoins you to treat women well, for they are your mothers, daughters and aunts.

~ *Prophet Muhammed*

All I know is that I am not a Marxist.

~ *Karl Marx*

Do you see now that your self-righteousness was nothing more than breeding and years of privilege? You know, we are one nation under a god. Yes, you were right. An angry, crack slinging god who decorates with bullets and spent condoms, a blind god whose eyes are just like yours.

~ *Solipsist by Henry Rollins*

If you talk to God, you are praying. If God talks to you, you have schizophrenia.

~ *Thomas Szasz*

It is not easy to find happiness in ourselves; it is not possible to find it elsewhere.

~ *Unknown*

To know is to be ignorant, not to know is the beginning of wisdom.

~ *J. Krishnamurthi*

When war is declared, truth is the first casualty.

~ *Arthur Ponsonby*

If you have one true friend you have more than your share.

~ *Thomas Fuller*

The more man meditates upon good thoughts; the better will be his world and the world at large.

~ *Confucius*

Never contend with a man who has nothing to lose.

~ *Baltasar Gracian*

The state has not the right to leave every man free to profess and embrace whatever religion he may desire.

~ *Pope Pius IX*

Passionate hatred can give meaning and purpose to an empty life. Thus people haunted by the purposelessness of their lives try to find a new content not only by dedicating themselves to a holy cause but also by nursing a fanatical grievance. A mass movement offers them unlimited opportunities for both.

~ *Eric Hoffer*

Safeguarding the rights of others is the most noble and beautiful end of a human being.

~ *Kahlil Gibran*

[Nationalism is] a set of beliefs taught to each generation in which the Motherland or the Fatherland is an object of veneration and becomes a burning cause for which one becomes willing to kill the children of other Motherlands or Fatherlands.

~ *Howard Zinn*

Government is actually the worst failure of civilized man. There has never been a really good one, and even those that are most tolerable are arbitrary, cruel, grasping and unintelligent.

~ *H. L. Mencken*

Being deeply loved by someone gives you strength; loving someone deeply gives you courage.

~ *Lao tzu*

You believe you are dying for the fatherland, you die for some industrialists.

~ *Anatole France*

The world is too dangerous to live in, not because of the people who do evil, but because of the people who sit and let it happen.

~ *Albert Einstein*

Giving money and power to government is like giving whiskey and car keys to teenage boys.

~ *P. J. O'Rourke*

Probably no nation is rich enough to pay for both war and education.

~ *Braham Flexner*

Rich gifts wax poor when givers prove unkind.

~ *William Shakespeare*

I'm not schizophrenia, and neither am I.

~ *Unknown*

A belief is not true because it is useful.

~ *Henri Frederic Amiel*

I love talking about the Kennedy assassination. The reason I do is because I'm fascinated by it. I'm fascinated that our government could lie to us so blatantly, so obviously for so long, and we do absolutely nothing about it.

~ *Bill Hicks*

Pain is certain, suffering is optional.

~ *Buddha*

There are three kinds of lies: lies, damn lies, and statistics.

~ *Benjamin Disraeli*

See how the boy is with his sister and you can know how the man will be with your daughter.

~ *Plains Lakota*

Fascism is capitalism in decay.

~ *Nikolai Lenin*

Americans used to roar like lions for liberty; now we bleat like sheep for security.

~ *Norman Vincent Peale*

The police are not here to create disorder. They're here to preserve disorder.

~ *Ex-Chicago Mayor Daley during the 1968 riots*

When did I realize I was God? Well, I was praying and I suddenly realized I was talking to myself.

~ *Peter O'Toole*

Whatever crushes individuality is despotism, by whatever name it may be called.

~ *John Stuart Mill*

The law is reason unaffected by desire.

~ *Aristotle*

The old forget. The young don't know.

~ *Japanese proverb*

Could a being create the fifty billion galaxies, each with two hundred billion stars, then rejoice in the smell of burning goat flesh?

~ *Ron Patterson*

Humanity has the stars in its future, and that future is too important to be lost under the burden of juvenile folly and ignorant superstition.

~ *Isaac Asimov*

The cynics are right nine times out of ten.

~ *H. L. Mencken*

I'm gayer than you are.

~ *Lapel Button*

In the end, we will remember not the words of our enemies, but the silence of our friends.

~ *Martin Luther King, Jr.*

Women who seek to be equal with men lack ambition.

~ *Timothy Leary*

I don't know that atheists should be considered citizens, nor should they be considered patriots. This is one nation under God.

~ *President George Bush, August 27, 1988*

The United States is in no sense founded upon the Christian doctrine.

~ *George Washington*

Oh Lord, please protect me from your followers!

~ *Lapel Button*

If you wish to experience peace, provide peace for another. If you wish to know that you are safe, cause others to know that they are safe. If you wish to better understand seemingly incomprehensible things, help another to better understand. If you wish to heal your own sadness or anger, seek to heal the sadness or anger of another. Those others are waiting for you now. They are looking to you for guidance, for help, for courage, for strength, for understanding, and for assurance at this hour. Most of all, they are looking to you for love.

~ *Dalai Lama*

Life is a tragedy full of joy.

~ *Bernard Malamud*

Beliefs are what divide people. Doubt unites them.

~ *Peter Ustinov*

Do not seek death. Death will find you. But seek the road which makes death a fulfillment.

~ *Dag Hammarskjöld*

The only excuse for God is that he doesn't exist.

~ *Stendhal*

Christianity makes suffering contagious.

~ *Nietzsche*

The wise man will love; all others will desire.

~ *Afranius*

Men make counterfeit money; in many more cases, money makes counterfeit men.

~ *Sydney J. Harris*

I don't give a *expletive deleted* what happens. I want you all to stonewall it, let them plead the Fifth Amendment, cover up or anything else, if it'll save it, save this plan. That's the whole point.

~ *Richard Nixon*

The exact contrary of what is generally believed is often the truth.

~ *Jean de la Bruyère*

College isn't the place to go for ideas.

~ *Helen Keller*

That best portion of a good man's life is his little, nameless, unremembered acts of kindness and of love.

~ *William Wordsworth*

The man who makes no mistakes does not usually make anything.

~ *Edward John Phelps*

May your fondest wish be granted.
~ *Traditional Chinese curse*

Truth is stranger than fiction, but it is because fiction is obliged to stick to possibilities; truth isn't.
~ *Mark Twain*

Crazy that you are, why do you promise yourself to live a long time, you who cannot count on a single day.
~ *Warning sign, Paris Catacombs*

Three things cannot be long hidden: the sun, the moon, and the truth.
~ *Buddha*

The shepherd drives the wolf from the sheep's throat, for which the sheep thanks the shepherd as his liberator, while the wolf denounces him for the same act as the destroyer of liberty.
~ *Abraham Lincoln*

Life is too short to waste in critical peep or cynic bark, quarrel or reprimand: It will soon be dark.
~ *Ralph Waldo Emerson*

A man, after he has brushed off the dust and chips of his life, will have left only the hard clean question: Was it good or was it evil? Have I done well or ill?
~ *John Steinbeck*

There is no adequate defense, except stupidity, against the impact of a new idea.
~ *Percy Williams Bridgeman*

Believe those who are seeking the truth; doubt those who find it.
~ *Andre Gide*

When your work speaks for itself, don't interrupt.
~ *Henry J. Kaiser*

It is amazing how complete is the delusion that beauty is goodness.
~ *Leo Tolstoy*

That's not a lie, it's a terminological inexactitude.
~ *Alexander Haig*

Truth is for the minority.
~ *Baltasar Gracián*

There's one way to find out if a man is honest, ask him. If he says, yes, you know he's a crook.
~ *Groucho Marx*

To obtain a man's opinion of you, make him mad.
~ *Oliver Wendell Holmes*

When I die, I hope to go to Heaven, whatever the Hell that is.
~ *Ayn Rand*

It is not enough to have a good mind; the main thing is to use it well.
~ *Rene Descartes*

I have no particular talent. I am merely inquisitive.
~ *Albert Einstein*

Peace hath higher tests of manhood than battle ever knew.
~ *John Greenleaf Whittier*

Laughter is the closest distance between two people.
~ *Victor Borge*

Life is fraught with opportunities to keep your mouth shut.

~ *Winston Churchill*

It's just a ride and we can change it any time we want. It's only a choice. No effort, no work, no job, no savings and money, a choice, right now, between fear and love. The eyes of fear want you to put bigger locks on your door, buy guns, close yourself off. The eyes of love instead see all of us as one.

~ *Bill Hicks*

Organic chemistry is the chemistry of carbon compounds. Biochemistry is the study of carbon compounds that crawl.

~ *Mike Adams*

So far as I can remember, there is not one word in the Gospels in praise of intelligence.

~ *Bertrand Russel*

The articles and dogmas of a religion are mind made things and if you cling to them and shut yourself up in a code made for you, you do not and cannot know the truth of the Spirit that lies beyond all codes and dogmas, wide and large and free.

~ *The Mother Mirra*

A new scientific truth does not triumph by convincing its opponents and making them see the light, but rather because its opponents eventually die out, and a new generation grows up that is familiar with it.

~ *Max Planc*

I prayed for twenty years but received no answer until I prayed with my legs.

~ *Frederick Douglass, escaped slave*

Whenever I hear anyone arguing for slavery, I feel a strong impulse to see it tried on him personally.

~ *Abraham Lincoln*

It is better to be feared than loved, if you cannot be both.

~ *Niccolo Machiavelli*

Politics is the art of looking for trouble, finding it everywhere, diagnosing it incorrectly, and applying the wrong remedies.

~ *Groucho Marx*

I use emotion for the many and reserve reason for the few.

~ *Adolf Hitler*

He who fights with monsters might take care lest he thereby become a monster. For if you gaze for long into an abyss, the abyss gazes also into you.

~ *Nietzsche*

When encountering a new philosophy or religion, do not convert, but rather assimilate.

~ *Shawn Mikula*

Women and cats will do as they please; men and dogs should relax and get used to the idea.

~ *Robert Heinlein*

The most incomprehensible thing about the universe is that it is comprehensible.

~ *Albert Einstein*

We are what we repeatedly do. Excellence, then, is not an act, but a habit.

~ *Aristotle*

You need only reflect that one of the best ways to get yourself a reputation as a dangerous citizen these days is to go about repeating the very phrases which our founding fathers used in the great struggle for independence.

~ *Attributed to Charles Austin Beard*

It is never right to do wrong or to requite wrong with wrong, or when we suffer evil to defend ourselves by doing evil in return.

~ *Socrates*

Everywhere is walking distance if you have the time.

~ *Steven Wright*

At the risk of seeming ridiculous, let me say that the true revolutionary is guided by great feelings of love. It is impossible to think of a genuine revolutionary lacking this quality.

~ *Ernesto 'Che' Guevara*

The questions remain the same. The answers are eternally variable.

~ *Unknown*

The only thing necessary for the triumph of evil is for good men to do nothing.

~ *Edmund Burke*

The way to heaven has no favorite. It is always with the good man.

~ *Lao tzu*

The citizen who sees his society's democratic clothes being worn out and does not cry it out, is not a patriot, but a traitor.

~ *Mark Twain*

Why is marijuana against the law? It grows naturally upon our planet. Doesn't the idea of making nature against the law seem to you a bit... unnatural? You know what I mean? It's nature. How do you make nature against the fucking law?

~ *Bill Hicks*

Happiness makes up in height for what it lacks in length.

~ *Robert Frost*

The liar's punishment is not in the least that he is not believed, but that he cannot believe anyone else.

~ *George Bernard Shaw*

Reality is that which, when you stop believing in it, doesn't go away.

~ *Philip K. Dick*

Wisdom is knowing what to do next. Virtue is doing it.

~ *David Starr Jordan*

As a child I understood how to give; I have forgotten this grace since I became civilized.

~ *Ohiyesa, Sioux*

Punishing honest mistakes stifles creativity. I want people moving and shaking the earth and they're going to make mistakes.

~ *Ross Perot*

Talk sense to a fool and he calls you foolish.

~ *Euripides*

Every generation laughs at the old fashions, but religiously follows the new.

~ *Henry David Thoreau*

Religion is the sign of the oppressed creature, the sentiment of a heartless world, and the soul of soulless conditions. It is the opium of the people.

~ *Karl Marx*

Those who hate and fight must stop themselves; otherwise it is not stopped.

~ *Spock, Day of the Dove*

A good government produces citizens distinguished for courage, love of justice, and every other good quality; a bad government makes them cowardly, rapacious, and the slave of every foul desire.

~ *Dionysius of Halicarnassus*

Absence of proof is not proof of absence.

~ *Michael Crichton*

Can anything be stupider than that a man has the right to kill me because he lives on the other side of a river and his ruler has a quarrel with mine, though I have not quarreled with him?

~ *Blaise Pascal*

Compassion is the basis of all morality.

~ *Arthur Schopenhauer*

Money may be the husk of many things, but not the kernel. It buys you food, but not appetite; medicine, but not health; acquaintances, but not friends; servants, but not loyalty; days of joy, but not peace or happiness.

~ *Henrik Ibsen*

I pay no attention to numbers; what matters is the people.

~ *Mother Teresa*

Were it left for me to decide whether we should have a government without newspapers, or newspapers without a government, I should not hesitate a moment to prefer the latter.

~ *Thomas Jefferson*

Whatever you do will be insignificant, but it is very important that you do it.

~ *Mohandas Gandhi*

Kindness is loving people more than they deserve.

~ *Joseph Joubert*

You can't have everything. Where would you put it?

~ *Steven Wright*

The existence of racism pains me. Hopefully, we may one day grow out of it, and some of the other ugly traditions and regressive myths our species continues to dabble in. Maybe then, our evolution won't be mainly technological.

~ *Ian Thomas*

The reward of a thing well done is to have done it.

~ *Ralph Waldo Emerson*

Don’t fail and try again, try everything and see what fails.

~ *David Keyes*

We are ever striving after what is forbidden, and coveting what is denied us.

~ *Ovid*

All violence, all that is dreary and repels, is not power, but the absence of power.

~ *Ralph Waldo Emerson*

When I was about twenty years old, I met an old pastor's wife who told me that when she was young and had her first child, she didn't believe in striking children, although spanking kids with a switch pulled from a tree was standard punishment at the time. But one day when her son was four or five, he did something that she felt warranted a spanking - the first of his life. - And she told him that he would have to go outside and find a switch for her to hit him with. The boy was gone a long time. And when he came back in, he was crying. He said to her, Mama, I couldn't find a switch, but here's a rock that you can throw at me. All of a sudden the mother understood how the situation felt from the child's point of view: that if my mother wants to hurt me, then it makes no difference what she does it with; she might as well do it with a stone. And the mother took the boy onto her lap and they both cried. - Then she laid the rock on a shelf in the kitchen to remind herself forever: never violence. And that is something I think everyone should keep in mind. Because violence begins in the nursery, one can raise children into violence.

~ *Astrid Lindgren*

I was asked to memorize what I did not understand; and, my memory being so good, it refused to be insulted in that manner.

~ *Aleister Crowley*

The keenest sorrow is to recognize ourselves as the sole cause of all our adversities.

~ *Sophocles*

Common sense is the collection of prejudices acquired by age eighteen.

~ *Albert Einstein*

The way to find what the mainstream will do tomorrow is to associate with the lunatic fringe today.

~ *Jean-Louis Gassee*

When ideas fail, words come in very handy.

~ *Johann Wolfgang von Goethe*

Religion has done love a great service by making it a sin.

~ *Anatole France*

Hell, there are no rules here; we're trying to accomplish something.

~ *Thomas Edison*

Superstition is a great enemy of man but bigotry is worse.

~ *Swami Vivekananda*

A jury consists of twelve persons chosen to decide who has the better lawyer.

~ *Robert Frost*

Whether you think that you can or that you can't, you are usually right.

~ *Henry Ford*

It is what we learn after we think we know it all that counts.

~ *John Wooden*

Our job is to give people not what they want, but what we decide they ought to have.

~ *Richard Salent, Former President CBS News*

Nature is not human hearted.

~ *Lao tzu*

History will have to record that the greatest tragedy of this period of social transition was not the strident clamor of the bad people, but the appalling silence of the good people.

~ *Martin Luther King, Jr.*

Scientific progress consists in the development of new concepts.

~ *Ernst Mayr*

As long as war is regarded as wicked, it will always have its fascination. When it is looked upon as vulgar it will cease to be popular.

~ *Oscar Wilde*

Silence is argument carried out by other means.

~ *Ernesto 'Che' Guevara*

You can pretend to be serious; you can't pretend to be witty.

~ *Sacha Guitry*

Two attitudes are all that is needed; do not harm anything, say and do things that make others happy.

~ *dreamslaughter*

In spite of everything I still believe that people are really good at heart.

~ *Anne Frank, holocaust victim*

The nationalist not only does not disapprove of atrocities committed by his own side, but he has a remarkable capacity for not even hearing about them.

~ *George Orwell*

Never mistake motion for action.

~ *Ernest Hemingway*

We keep, in science, getting a more and more sophisticated view of our essential ignorance.

~ *Warren Weaver*

When you think of the long and gloomy history of man, you will find more hideous crimes have been committed in the name of obedience than have ever been committed in the name of rebellion.

~ *C. P. Snow*

Why is propaganda so much more successful when it stirs up hatred than when it tries to stir up friendly feeling?

~ *Bertrand Russell*

Although the time of death is approaching me, I am not afraid of dying and going to Hell or what would be considerably worse going to the popularized version of Heaven. I expect death to be nothingness and, for removing me from all possible fears of death, I am thankful to atheism.

~ *Isaac Asimov*

Scientific criticism has no nobler task than to shatter false beliefs.

~ *Ludwig von Mises*

To the Puritan all things are impure.

~ *D. H. Lawrence*

Everything that divides men, everything that separates or herds men together in categories, is a sin against humanity.

~ *José Martí*

The cruelest lies are often told in silence.

~ *Robert Louis Stevenson*

The only thing we learn from history is that we learn nothing from history.

~ *Friedrich Hegel*

There must be no barriers for freedom of inquiry. There is no place for dogma in science. The scientist is free, and must be free to ask any question, to doubt any assertion, to seek for any evidence, to correct any errors.

~ *Robert Oppenheimer*

Nature does not hurry, yet everything is accomplished.

~ *Lao tzu*

It is by will alone that I set my mind in motion.

~ *Frank Herbert*

The ideals which have always shone before me and filled me with the joy of living are goodness, beauty, and truth. To make a goal of comfort or happiness has never appealed to me; a system of ethics built on this basis would be sufficient only for a herd of cattle.

~ *Albert Einstein*

What should it matter that one bowl is dark and the other pale, if each is good of design and serves its purpose well?

~ *Hopi*

History teaches us that men and nations behave wisely once they have exhausted all other alternatives.

~ *Abba Eban*

He who has a thousand friends has not a friend to spare, while he who has one enemy shall meet him everywhere.

~ *Ralph Waldo Emerson*

Heaven goes by favor; if it went by merit, you would stay out and your dog would go in.

~ *Mark Twain*

Life is made up of marble and mud.

~ *Nathaniel Hawthorne*

Death in all its shapes is hateful to unhappy man, but the worst is death of hunger.

~ *Homer*

When dealing with the insane, it is best to pretend to be sane.

~ *Herman Hesse*

I know you've come to kill me. Shoot, coward, you're only going to kill a man.

~ *Ernesto 'Che' Guevara*

The illegal we do immediately. The unconstitutional takes a bit longer.

~ *Henry Kissinger*

The surest way to corrupt a youth is to instruct him to hold in higher esteem those who think alike than those who think differently.

~ *Nietzsche*

The victor will never be asked if he told the truth.

~ *Adolf Hitler*

Justice is incidental to law and order.

~ *J. Edgar Hoover*

It is more shameful to mistrust one's friends than to be deceived by them.

~ *Francois Duc de la Rochefoucauld*

It would be absurd if we did not understand both angels and devils, since we invented them.

~ *John Steinbeck*

Writing science fiction for about a penny a word is no way to make a living, if you really want to make a million, the quickest way is to start your own religion.

~ *L. Ron Hubbard*

Yes, we love peace, but we are not willing to take wounds for it, as we are for war.

~ *John Andrew Holmes*

A little rebellion now and then is a good thing.

~ *Thomas Jefferson*

When the horse dies, dismount.

~ *Unknown*

You have the capacity to choose what you think about. If you choose to think about past hurts, you will continue to feel bad. While it's true you can't change the effect past influences had on you once, you can change the effect they have on you now.

~ *Gary McKay PhD*

Not to know is bad. Not to want to know is worse. Not to hope is unthinkable. Not to care is unforgiving.

~ *Nigerian saying*

If you tell the truth, you don't have to remember anything.

~ *Mark Twain*

Let the human mind loose. It must be loosed; it will be loose, superstition and despotism cannot confine it.

~ *John Adams*

It is not in the stars to hold our destiny but in ourselves.
~ *William Shakespeare*

All I want is a warm bed and a kind word and unlimited power.
~ *Ashleigh Brilliant*

The basis of optimism is sheer terror.
~ *Oscar Wilde*

A leader is one who, out of madness or goodness, volunteers to take upon himself the woe of the people. There are few men so foolish, hence the erratic quality of leadership in the world.
~ *John Updike*

The scars of others should teach us caution.
~ *Saint Jerome*

It is not easy to see how the more extreme forms of nationalism can long survive when men have seen the Earth in its true perspective as a single small globe against the stars.
~ *Arthur C. Clarke*

Consistency is the last resort of the unimaginative.
~ *Oscar Wilde*

In writing a novel, when in doubt, have two guys come through the door with guns.
~ *Raymond Chandler*

The genius of you Americans is that you never make clear-cut stupid moves, only complicated stupid moves, which make us wonder at the possibility that there may be something to them we are missing.
~ *Gamel Abdel Nasser*

If one morning I walked on top of the water across the Potomac River, the headline that afternoon would read; 'President Can't Swim.'

~ *Lyndon B. Johnson*

I learned long ago never to wrestle with a pig. You get dirty, and besides, the pig likes it.

~ *George Bernard Shaw*

It is a man's own mind, not his enemy or foe that lures him to evil ways.

~ *Buddha*

I'd like to live as a poor man with lots of money.

~ *Pablo Picasso*

What you do not wish upon yourself, extend not to others.

~ *Confucius*

Thinking is the talking of the soul with itself.

~ *Plato*

Everyone hears only what he understands.

~ *Johann Wolfgang von Goethe*

Even if you are on the right track, you'll get run over if you just sit there.

~ *Will Rogers*

A gentleman is a man who can play the accordion but doesn't.

~ *Unknown*

When the only tool you have is a hammer, every problem begins to resemble a nail.

~ *Abraham Maslow*

In heaven all the interesting people are missing.

~ *Nietzsche*

The best way to keep the home fires burning is with chips from our own shoulders.

~ *Unknown*

You can't be a real country unless you have a beer and an airline. It helps if you have some kind of a football team, or some nuclear weapons, but at the very least you need a beer.

~ *Frank Zappa*

Who is a wise man? He who learns of all men.

~ *The Talmud*

I have yet to see any problem, however complicated, which, when you looked at it in the right way, did not become still more complicated.

~ *Poul Anderson*

To confine our attention to terrestrial matters would be to limit the human spirit.

~ *Stephen Hawking*

Government exists to protect us from each other. Where government has gone beyond its limits is in deciding to protect us from ourselves.

~ *Ronald Reagan*

The end of law is, not to abolish or restrain, but to preserve and enlarge freedom.

~ *John Locke*

What sane person could live in this world and not be crazy?

~ *Ursula K. LeGuin*

Everyone wants to be Cary Grant. Even I want to be Cary Grant.

~ *Cary Grant*

You can't build a reputation on what you are going to do.

~ *Henry Ford*

Money couldn't buy friends, but you get a better class of enemy.

~ *Spike Mulligan*

Our elections are free; it's in the results where eventually we pay.

~ *Bill Stern*

Democracy becomes a government of bullies tempered by editors.

~ *Ralph Waldo Emerson*

If God dwells inside us like some people say, I sure hope he likes enchiladas, cuz that's what he's getting.

~ *Jack Handey*

A computer lets you make more mistakes faster than any invention in human history, with the possible exceptions of handguns and tequila.

~ *Mitch Ratliffe*

It ain't those parts of the Bible that I can't understand that bother me, it's the parts that I do understand.

~ *Mark Twain*

Time is the coin of your life. It is the only coin you have, and only you can determine how it will be spent. Be careful lest you let other people spend it for you.

~ *Carl Sandburg*

There was a time when a fool and his money were soon parted, but now it happens to everybody.

~ *Adlai Stevenson*

No man who needs a monument ever ought to have one.

~ *Nathaniel Hawthorne*

Human salvation lies in the hands of the creatively maladjusted.

~ *Martin Luther King, Jr.*

Your religion was written on tablets of stone, ours was written on our hearts.

~ *Chief Seattle*

Enlighten the people generally, and tyranny and oppressions of body and mind will vanish like evil spirits at the dawn of day.

~ *Thomas Jefferson*

When the rich wage war it's the poor who die.

~ *Jean-Paul Sartre*

Crash programs fail because they are based on theory that, with nine women pregnant, you can get a baby a month.

~ *Wernher von Braun*

The price of monopoly is upon every occasion the highest which can be got.

~ *Adam Smith*

A military operation involves deception. Even though you are competent, appear to be incompetent. Though effective, appear to be ineffective.

~ *Sun tzu*

It does not prove a thing to be right because the majority say it is so.

~ *Friedrich von Schiller*

Violence is the last refuge of the incompetent.

~ *Isaac Asimov*

If you want to make an apple pie from scratch, you must first create the universe.

~ *Carl Sagan*

Tip the world over on its side and everything loose will land in Los Angeles.

~ *Frank Lloyd Wright*

If there is a fifty-fifty chance that something can go wrong, then nine times out of ten it will.

~ *Paul Harvey*

Science commits suicide when it adopts a creed.

~ *Thomas Huxley*

A good man would prefer to be defeated than to defeat injustice by evil means.

~ *Sallust*

Be not ashamed of mistakes and thus make them crimes.

~ *Confucius*

Nationalism is an infantile sickness. It is the measles of the human race.

~ *Albert Einstein*

He who is dying of hunger must be fed rather than taught.

~ *Saint Thomas Aquinas*

Even peace may be purchased at too high a price.

~ *Ben Franklin*

He of whom many are afraid ought to fear many.

~ *Sir Francis Bacon*

Political history is largely an account of mass violence and of the expenditure of vast resources to cope with mythical fears and hopes.

~ *Murray Edelman*

Pride grows in the human heart like lard on a pig.

~ *Aleksandr Solzhenitsyn*

Integrity is the value we set on ourselves.

~ *James E. Faust*

Any sufficiently advanced technology is indistinguishable from magic.

~ *Arthur C. Clarke*

Ninety percent of everything is crap.

~ *Theodore Sturgeon*

It is a blessing to die for a cause, because you can so easily die for nothing.

~ *Andrew Young*

Modern morality and manners suppress all natural instincts, keep people ignorant of the facts of nature and make them fighting drunk on bogey tales.

~ *Aleister Crowley*

I don't know with what weapons World War III will be fought, but World War IV will be fought with sticks and stones.

~ *Albert Einstein*

In the mountains of truth, you never climb in vain. Either you already reach a higher point today, or you exercise your strength in order to be able to climb higher tomorrow.

~ *Nietzsche*

Plenty has made me poor.

~ *Ovid*

The activist is not the man who says the river is dirty. The activist is the man who cleans up the river.

~ *Ross Perot*

The cure for boredom is curiosity. There is no cure for curiosity.

~ *Dorothy Parker*

No benevolent man ever lost altogether the fruits of his benevolence.

~ *Adam Smith*

Crooked things may be as stiff and unflexible as straight: and men may be as positive in error as in truth.

~ *John Locke*

A straight line may be the shortest distance between two points, but it is by no means the most interesting.

~ *Dr. Who*

A goal without a plan is just a wish.

~ *Antoine de Saint-Exupery*

The most exciting phrase to hear in science, the one that heralds new discoveries, is not 'Eureka! I found it!' But 'That's funny.'

~ *Isaac Asimov*

We owe almost all our knowledge not to those who have agreed but to those who have differed.

~ *Charles C. Colton*

Formerly, when religion was strong and science weak, men mistook magic for medicine; now, when science is strong and religion weak, men mistake medicine for magic.

~ *Thomas Szasz*

Never express yourself more clearly than you think.

~ *Neils Bohr*

Patriotism is the principle that will justify the training of wholesale murderers.

~ *Leo Tolstoy*

Charity that is concealed appeases the wrath of God.

~ *Prophet Muhammad*

Whoever undertakes to set himself up as judge in the field of truth and knowledge is shipwrecked by the laughter of the Gods.

~ *Albert Einstein*

Time sneaks up on you like a windshield on a bug.

~ *Jon Lithgow*

When poverty comes in the door, love leaps out the window.

~ *John Clark*

I searched through rebellion, drugs, diets, mysticism, religions, intellectualism and much more, only to begin to find that truth is basically simple; and feels good, clean and right.

~ *Chick Corea*

Would you sing 'Krishna bless America' or pledge allegiance to 'One nation under Allah?' If not, would that make you unpatriotic?

~ *Chris Lee*

Society often forgives the criminal, but it never forgives the dreamer.

~ *Oscar Wilde*

We seem to have a compulsion these days to bury time capsules in order to give those people living in the next century or so some idea of what we are like. I have prepared one of my own. I have placed some rather large samples of dynamite, gunpowder, and nitroglycerin. My time capsule is set to go off in the year three thousand. It will show them what we are really like.

~ *Alfred Hitchcock*

This crime called blasphemy was invented by priests for the purpose of defending doctrines not able to take care of themselves.

~ *Robert G. Ingersoll*

Millions of Germans had absolute faith in Hitler. Millions of Russians had faith in Stalin. Millions of Chinese had faith in Mao. Billions have had faith in imaginary gods.

~ *Steve Allen*

It is the business of the future to be dangerous. The major advances in civilization are processes that all but wreck the societies in which they occur.

~ *Alfred North Whitehead*

We shall some day catch an abstract truth by the tail, and then we shall have our religion and our immortality.

~ *Henry Brooks Adams*

Forget injuries; never forget kindnesses.

~ *Confucius*

No matter what side of an argument you're on, you always find some people on your side that you wish were on the other side.

~ *Jascha Heifetz*

A lie has speed, but truth has endurance.

~ *Edgar J. Mohn*

Heavier than air flying machines are impossible.

~ *Lord Kelvin, president, Royal Society, 1895*

Being a hero is about the shortest-lived profession on earth.

~ *Will Rogers*

Not by force of arms are civilizations held together, but by subtle threads of moral and intellectual principle.

~ *Russell Kirk*

I imagined some horrible things in my life, a few of which actually occurred.

~ *Ben Franklin*

It is better to know some of the questions than all of the answers.

~ *James Thurber*

Discretion in speech is more than eloquence.

~ *Sir Francis Bacon*

The right things to do are those that keep our violence in abeyance; the wrong things are those that bring it to the fore.

~ *Robert J. Sawyer*

To someone seeking power, the poorest man is the most useful.

~ *Sallust*

All things are only transitory.

~ *Johann Wolfgang von Goethe*

He who lives without folly is not as wise as he thinks.

~ *Francois Duc de la Rochefoucauld*

It is easy enough to be friendly to one's friends. But to befriend the one who regards himself as your enemy is the quintessence of true religion. The other is mere business.

~ *Mohandas Gandhi*

The diamond cannot be polished without friction, nor the man perfected without trials.

~ *Chinese Proverb*

If child molestation is actually your concern, how come we don't see Bradley tanks knocking down Catholic churches?

~ *Bill Hicks, 1993, referencing the Waco siege*

Moral indignation: jealousy with a halo.

~ *H. G. Wells*

People with advantages are loath to believe that they just happen to be people with advantages.

~ *C. Wright Mills*

I am enough of an artist to draw freely upon my imagination. Imagination is more important than knowledge. Knowledge is limited. Imagination encircles the world.

~ *Albert Einstein*

I have to respect him for at least having a logically coherent reason for arriving at the totally wrong conclusion.

~ *Unknown*

You find as you look around the world that every single bit of progress in humane feeling, every improvement in the criminal law, every step toward the diminution of war, every step toward better treatment of the colored races, or every mitigation of slavery, every moral progress that there has been in the world, has been consistently opposed by the organized churches of the world. I say quite deliberately that the Christian religion, as organized in its churches, has been and still is the principal enemy of moral progress in the world.

~ *Bertrand Russell*

If we worry too much about ourselves, we won't have time for others.

~ *Mother Teresa*

And death makes equal the high and low.

~ *John Heywood*

When you are content to be simply yourself and don't compare or compete, everybody will respect you.

~ *Lao tzu*

A little bit is infinitely more than none at all.

~ *Pat Keyes*

Follow your inclinations with due regard to the policeman round the corner.

~ *William Somerset Maugham*

When the stomach is full, it is easy to talk of fasting.

~ *Saint Jerome*

Before you speak, ask yourself is it kind, is it necessary, is it true, does it improve on the silence?

~ *Shirdi Sai Bab*

Everything of importance has been said before by somebody who did not discover it.

~ *Alfred North Whitehead*

If we have to give up either religion or education, we should give up education.

~ *William Jennings Bryan*

To live a pure unselfish life, one must count nothing as one's own in the midst of abundance.

~ *Buddha*

The good Christian should beware of mathematicians and all those who make empty prophecies. The danger already exists that mathematicians have made a covenant with the devil to darken the spirit and confine man in the bonds of Hell.

~ *Saint Augustine*

The color of the skin makes no difference. What is good and just for one is good and just for the other. And the Great Spirit made all men brothers.

~ *White Shield, Arikara*

When the gods wish to punish us, they answer our prayers.

~ *Oscar Wilde*

Those who see and feel beyond illusion have acquired a far greater gift than could ever be derived from studying scripture and philosophy books, for these were meant only to guide the blind.

~ *Shawn Mikula*

Secular schools can never be tolerated because such schools have no religious instruction, and a general moral instruction without a religious foundation is built on air; consequently, all character training and religion must be derived from faith ... we need believing people.

~ *Adolf Hitler*

Do what you wish, as long as it harms no one; that includes yourself.

~ *Wiccan Creed*

Charity is a duty unto every Muslim. He who has not the means thereto let him do a good act or abstain from an evil one. That is his charity.

~ *Prophet Muhammad*

When angry, count to ten before you speak, when very angry, a hundred.

~ *Thomas Jefferson*

Did you ever notice how in the Bible when God needed to punish someone, make an example, or whenever God needed a killing he sent an angel? Have you ever wondered what a creature like that must be like? Your whole existence praising your God but always with one wing dipped in blood. Would you ever really want to see an angel?

~ *Thomas, The Prophecy*

Nothing does reason more right, than the coolness of those that offer it; for truth often suffers more by the heat of its defenders, than from the arguments of its opposers.

~ *William Penn*

Sometime they'll give a war and nobody will come.

~ *Carl Sandburg*

I like your Christ; I do not like your Christians. Your Christians are so unlike your Christ.

~ *Mohandas Gandhi*

Theology is never any help; it is searching in a dark cellar at midnight for a black cat that isn't there. Theologians can persuade themselves of anything.

~ *Robert Heinlein*

Answer not a fool according to his folly, lest thou be like unto him.

~ *Proverbs 26:4*

All righteous words and righteous deeds spring from knowledge and wisdom.

~ *Zarathushtra*

Don't worry about people stealing an idea. If it's original, you will have to ram it down their throats.

~ *Howard Aiken*

This monkey mythology of Darwin is the cause of permissiveness, promiscuity, prophylactics, perversions, pregnancies, abortions, porno-therapy, pollution, poisoning and proliferation of crimes of all types.

~ *Judge Braswell Dean*

It is a miracle that curiosity survives formal education.

~ *Albert Einstein*

Positive anything is better than negative nothing.

~ *Elbert Hubbard*

To see what is right, and not to do it, is want of courage or of principle.

~ *Confucius*

What is the use of a house if you haven't got a tolerable planet to put it on?

~ *Henry David Thoreau*

I consider Christian theology to be one of the greatest disasters of the human race.

~ *Alfred North Whitehead*

Where it is a duty to worship the sun, it is pretty sure to be a crime to examine the laws of heat.

~ *John Morley*

I despise mystics; they fancy themselves so deep, when they aren't even superficial.

~ *Nietzsche*

Few men have virtue to withstand the highest bidder.

~ *George Washington*

The truth is cruel, but it can be loved, and it makes free those who have loved it.

~ *George Santayana*

Never run after your own hat, others will be delighted to do it; why spoil their fun.

~ *Mark Twain*

Jesus was all right, but his disciples were thick and ordinary. It's them twisting it that ruins it for me.

~ *John Lennon*

Could a greater miracle take place than for us to look through each other's eyes for an instant?

~ *Henry David Thoreau*

Faith is believing something you know ain't true.

~ *Samuel Clemens*

People demand freedom of speech to make up for the freedom of thought, which they avoid.

~ *Søren Kierkegaard*

Have more than thou showest, speak less than thou knowest.

~ *William Shakespeare*

Liberties are not given; they are taken.

~ *Aldous Huxley*

He who joyfully marches to music in rank and file has already earned my contempt. He has been given a large brain by mistake, since for him the spinal cord would fully suffice. This disgrace to civilization should be done away with at once.

~ *Albert Einstein*

They that can give up essential liberty to obtain a little temporary safety deserve neither liberty nor safety.

~ *Ben Franklin*

No man is good enough to govern another man without that other's consent.

~ *Abraham Lincoln*

Histories are more full of examples of the fidelity of dogs than of friends.

~ *Alexander Pope*

Never be deceived that the rich will allow you to vote away their wealth.

~ *Lucy Parsons*

All truths are easy to understand once they are discovered; the point is to discover them.

~ *Galileo Galilei*

There was once a man who did not like his footprints. His teacher told him to sit on the ground and rest and the footprints would disappear, for if he did not run, he would leave no mark, and if he could face the darkness, there would be no shadow. But this man had to run and so was chased by the footprints of his actions, and the shadows of his past.

~ *Vanishing Son*

Purity and impurity depend on oneself. No one can purify another.

~ *Buddha*

I'm not against the police; I'm just afraid of them.

~ *Alfred Hitchcock*

War will never cease until babies begin to come into the world with larger cerebrums and smaller adrenal glands.

~ *H. L. Mencken*

An error can never become true however many times you repeat it, truth can never be wrong even if no one hears it.

~ *Mohandas Gandhi*

I think this is the most extraordinary collection of talent, of human knowledge, that has ever been gathered at the White House; with the possible exception of when Thomas Jefferson dined alone.

~ *John F. Kennedy, honoring Nobel Prize winners*

Selling eternal life is an unbeatable business, with no customers ever asking for their money back after the goods are not delivered.

~ *Victor J. Stenger*

All men are caught in an inescapable network of mutuality.

~ *Martin Luther King, Jr.*

I never learned from a man who agreed with me.

~ *Robert Heinlein*

Anger is as a stone cast into a wasp's nest.

~ *Malabar proverb*

I have no further use for America. I wouldn't go back there if Jesus Christ was President.

~ *Charlie Chaplin*

No, I don't do drugs anymore, either. But I'll tell you something about drugs. I used to do drugs, but I'll tell you something honestly about drugs, honestly, and I know it's not a very popular idea, you don't hear it very often anymore, but it is the truth: I had a great time doing drugs. Sorry. Never murdered anyone, never robbed anyone, never raped anyone, never beat anyone, never lost a job, a car, a house, a wife or kids, laughed my ass off, and went about my day.

~ *Bill Hicks*

If I were two faced, would I be wearing this one?

~ *Abraham Lincoln*

Perfect kindness acts without thinking of kindness.

~ *Lao tzu*

Just think of the tragedy of teaching children not to doubt.

~ *Clarence Darrow*

The God of the Bible is a moral monstrosity.

~ *Rev. Henry Ward Beecher*

The opinion of ten-thousand men is of no value if none of them know anything about the subject.

~ *Marcus Aurelius*

The idea that there is a God who rewards and punishes, and who can reward, if he so wishes, the meanest and vilest of the human race, so that he will be eternally happy, and can punish the best of the human race, so that he will be eternally miserable; is subversive of all morality.

~ *Robert G. Ingersoll*

The fault dear Brutus, is not in our stars, but in ourselves, that we are underlings.

~ *William Shakespeare*

It is absurd to divide people into good and bad. People are either charming or tedious.

~ *Oscar Wilde*

By means of shrewd lies, unremittingly repeated, it is possible to make people believe that heaven is hell, and hell heaven. The greater the lie, the more readily it will be believed.

~ *Adolf Hitler*

I want to know the truth, however perverted that may sound.

~ *Stephen Wolfram*

Most people drive thru life with the parking brake on.

~ *Lance Bradley*

Truth is living, it is not static, and the mind that would discover truth must also be living, not burdened with knowledge or experience.

~ *J. Krishnamurthi*

If everyone demanded peace instead of another television set, then there'd be peace.

~ *John Lennon*

Advertising reaches out to touch the fantasy part of people's lives. And you know, most people's fantasies are pretty sad.

~ *Frederik Pohl*

It's not getting any smarter out there. You have to come to terms with stupidity and make it work for you.

~ *Frank Zappa*

A witty saying proves nothing.

~ *Voltaire*

It's not what you don't know that hurts you. It's what you know that just isn't so.

~ *Satchel Paige*

A free society is one where it is safe to be unpopular.

~ *Adlai Stevenson*

Treat a work of art like a prince: let it speak to you first.

~ *Arthur Schopenhauer*

As a very important source of strength and security, cherish public credit. One method of preserving it is to use it as sparingly as possible.

~ *George Washington*

Wandering in a vast forest at night, I have only a faint light to guide me. A stranger appears and says to me: 'my friend, you should blow out your candle in order to find your way more clearly.' This stranger is a theologian.

~ *Denis Diderot*

It has become appallingly obvious that our technology has exceeded our humanity.

~ *Albert Einstein*

If a man really believes that God once upheld slavery; that he commanded soldiers to kill women and babes; that he persecuted for opinion's sake; that he will punish forever, and that he hates an unbeliever, the effect in my judgment will be bad. It always has been bad. This belief built the dungeons of the Inquisition. This belief made the Puritan murder the Quaker.

~ *Robert G. Ingersoll*

I do not read advertisements. I would spend all of my time wanting things.

~ *Franz Kafka*

Don't join the book burners.

~ *Dwight D. Eisenhower*

To date, despite the efforts of millions of true believers to support this myth, there is no more evidence for the Judeo-Christian god than any of the gods on Mount Olympus.

~ *Joseph Daleiden*

Free from desire, you realize the mystery. Caught in desire, you see only the manifestations.

~ *Tao Te Ching*

In cyberspace, the first Amendment is a local ordinance.

~ *John Perry Barlow*

The biggest conspiracy of all is the claim that there are no conspiracies!

~ *Michael Rivero*

The death of dogma is the birth of morality.
~ *Immanuel Kant*

If all else fails, immortality can always be assured by spectacular error.
~ *John Kenneth Galbraith*

It is the beautiful bird that gets the cage.
~ *Chinese proverb*

Few men desire liberty: The majority are satisfied with a just master.
~ *Sallust*

Skepticism, like chastity, should not be relinquished too readily.
~ *George Santayana*

Truth never damages a cause that is just.
~ *Mohandas Gandhi*

Knowledge is like a garden: if it is not cultivated, it cannot be harvested.
~ *Guinean saying*

Always forgive your enemies, nothing annoys them so much.
~ *Oscar Wilde*

Too often we enjoy the comfort of opinion without the discomfort of thought.
~ *John F. Kennedy*

If there was a god, he wouldn't let a guy walk right up and shoot you in the face now would he? That's right, now you get the picture. Truth burns doesn't it?
~ *Henry Rollins*

This country, with its institutions, belongs to the people who inhabit it. Whenever they shall grow weary of the existing government, they can exercise their constitutional right of amending it, or exercise their revolutionary right to overthrow it.

~ *Abraham Lincoln*

Humankind has not woven the web of life. We are but one thread within it. Whatever we do to the web, we do to ourselves. All things are bound together. All things connect.

~ *Chief Seattle*

If you believe in the existence of fairies at the bottom of the garden you are deemed fit for the bin. If you believe in parthenogenesis, ascension, transubstantiation and all the rest of it, you are deemed fit to govern the country.

~ *Jonathan Meades*

Gentlemen, you can't fight in here! This is the War Room!

~ *Dr. Strangelove*

I know of no crime that has not been defended by the church, in one form or other. The church is not a pioneer; it accepts a new truth, last of all, and only when denial has become useless.

~ *Robert G. Ingersoll*

The human race has one really effective weapon, and that is laughter.

~ *Mark Twain*

Neither fire nor wind, birth nor death can erase our good deeds.

~ *Buddha*

One of the symptoms of an approaching nervous breakdown is the belief that one's work is terribly important.

~ *Bertrand Russell*

In general the art of government consists in taking as much money as possible from one class of citizens to give to the other.

~ *Voltaire*

Ignorance is not lack of information about facts; ignorance is unawareness of the total process itself.

~ *J. Krishnamurthi*

Heroism on command, senseless violence, and all the loathsome nonsense that goes by the name of patriotism; how passionately I hate them!

~ *Albert Einstein*

What lies behind us and what lies before us are tiny matters compared to what lies within us.

~ *Oliver Wendell Holmes*

We cannot learn without pain.

~ *Aristotle*

Being president is like being a jackass in a hailstorm. There's nothing to do but to stand there and take it.

~ *Lyndon B. Johnson*

I have no country to fight for; my country is the earth, and I am a citizen of the world.

~ *Eugene V. Debs*

A nation is a society united by a delusion about its ancestry and by common hatred of its neighbors.

~ *William R. Inge*

Cast aside those who liken godliness to whimsy and who try to combine their greed for wealth with their desire for a happy afterlife.

~ *Kahlil Gibran*

He, who opens a school door, closes a prison.

~ *Victor Hugo*

The history of liberty is a history of resistance. The history of liberty is a history of limitations of governmental power, not the increase of it.

~ *Woodrow Wilson*

Ancient Egyptians believed that upon death they would be asked two questions and their answers would determine whether they could continue their journey in the afterlife. The first question was: Did you bring joy? The second was: Did you find joy?

~ *Leo Buscaglia*

If we do not like the world the way it is, then it is because we are not okay the way we are.

~ *deeshan*

It is your business, when the wall next door catches fire.

~ *Horace*

Life can only be understood backwards, but it must be lived forwards.

~ *Søren Kierkegaard*

Be polite to all, but intimate with few.

~ *Thomas Jefferson*

Wise men don't need advice; fools don't take it.

~ *Ben Franklin*

Noble people understand righteousness; petty people understand self-interest.

~ *Confucius*

Heaven, as conventionally conceived, is a place so inane, so dull, so useless, so miserable, that no-body has ever ventured to describe a whole day in heaven, though plenty of people have described a day at the seaside.

~ *George Bernard Shaw*

He who helps his fellow creature in need, and he who helps the oppressed, him will god help in the day of travail.

~ *Prophet Muhammad*

The sinews of war: unlimited money.

~ *Cicero*

Once you have seen certain things, you can't un-see them, and seeing nothing is as political an act as seeing something.

~ *Arundhati Roy*

Translate 'Allah'.

~ *Bumper Sticker*

There's no way to rule innocent men. The only power any government has is the power to crack down on criminals. Well, when there aren't enough criminals, one makes them. One declares so many things to be a crime that it becomes impossible for men to live without breaking laws.

~ *Ayn Rand*

The clearest sign of wisdom is continued cheerfulness.

~ *Montaigne*

Science is always discovering odd scraps of magical wisdom and making a tremendous fuss about its cleverness.

~ *Aleister Crowley*

The game of life is the game of boomerangs. Our thoughts, deeds and words return to us sooner or later, with astounding accuracy.

~ *Florence Shinn*

They said I was the greatest pitcher they ever saw; I couldn't understand why they couldn't give me no justice.

~ *Satchel Paige*

A conservative government is an organized hypocrisy.

~ *Benjamin Disraeli*

If a free society cannot help the many who are poor, it cannot save the few who are rich.

~ *John F. Kennedy*

Judging from the main portions of the history of the world, so far, justice is always in jeopardy.

~ *Walt Whitman*

Mistakes are the portals of discovery.

~ *James Joyce*

Tis better to remain silent and be thought a fool, than open one's mouth and remove all doubt.

~ *Samuel Johnson*

If a country is governed with tolerance, the people are comfortable and honest. If a country is governed with repression, the people are depressed and crafty.

~ *Tao Te Ching*

On the sixth day, God created man. On the seventh day, man returned the favor.
~ *Unknown*

Just as there can be no peace without order so there can be no order without justice.
~ *Pope Pius XII*

Be silent as to services you have rendered, but speak of favors you have received.
~ *Seneca*

If you fall from a tree, leave your anger on the branch.
~ *Unknown*

Wisdom outweighs any wealth.
~ *Sophocles*

The people, when they have been unchecked, have been as unjust, tyrannical, brutal, barbarous, and cruel as any king or senate possessed of uncontrollable power. The majority has eternally, and without exception, usurped over the rights of the minority.
~ *John Adams*

Conceit, arrogance, and egotism are the essentials of patriotism.
~ *Emma Goldman*

What I say is that 'just' or 'right' means nothing but what is in the interest of the stronger party.
~ *Plato*

I do not believe in immortality of the individual, and I consider ethics to be an exclusively human concern with no superhuman authority behind it.
~ *Albert Einstein*

The cause of all miseries from which we suffer is desire.

~ *Swami Vivekananda*

In taking revenge, a man is but even with his enemy; but in passing it over, he is superior.

~ *Sir Francis Bacon*

For God hates utterly, the bray of bragging tongues.

~ *Sophocles*

It is a sobering thought, for example, that when Mozart was my age, he had been dead for two years.

~ *Tom Lehrer*

The superpowers often behave like two heavily armed blind men feeling their way around a room, each believing himself in mortal peril from the other, whom he assumes to have perfect vision. Each tends to ascribe to the other side a consistency, foresight and coherence that its own experience belies. Of course, even two blind men can do enormous damage to each other, not to speak of the room.

~ *Henry Kissinger*

In a mad world, only the mad are sane.

~ *Akiro Kurosawa*

Why are the people starving? Because the rulers eat up the money in taxes. Therefore, the people are starving.

~ *Lao tzu*

Never doubt that a small group of thoughtful committed citizens can change the world; indeed, it is the only thing that ever has.

~ *Margaret Mead*

The real and complete liberation of mankind is the great aim, the sublime end of history.

~ *Mikhail A. Bakunin*

The object of the state is always the same: to limit the individual, to tame him, to subordinate him, to subjugate him.

~ *Max Stirner*

We can have democracy in this country, or we can have great wealth concentrated in the hands of a few, but we can't have both.

~ *Louis Brandeis*

America is the only country that went from barbarism to decadence without civilization in between.

~ *Oscar Wilde*

Do not weep; do not wax indignant. Understand.

~ *Baruch Spinoza*

The liberals can understand everything but people who don't understand them.

~ *Lenny Bruce*

It will yet be the proud boast of women that they never contributed a line to the Bible.

~ *George W. Foote*

The distinctive signs of true religion are goodwill, love truthfulness, purity, nobility of feeling and kindness.

~ *Buddha*

If you realize that all things change, there is nothing you will try to hold on to. If you aren't afraid of dying, there is nothing you can't achieve.

~ *Tao Te Ching*

Religion is what keeps the poor from murdering the rich.

~ *Napoleon*

Beauty is eternity gazing at itself in the mirror.

~ *Kahlil Gibran*

Nothing is worth more than this day.

~ *Johann Wolfgang von Goethe*

Fear is the foundation of most governments.

~ *John Adams*

The bible consists of six admonishments to homosexuals and three hundred and sixty-two admonishments to heterosexuals. That doesn't mean that god doesn't love heterosexuals, just that they need more supervision.

~ *Lynn Lavner*

Education is when you read the fine print. Experience is what you get if you don't.

~ *Pete Seeger*

The unclouded eye is better, no matter what it sees.

~ *Frank Herbert*

I would not be satisfied to have my kids choose to be religious without trying to argue them out of it, just as I would not be satisfied to have them decide to smoke regularly or engage in any other practice I considered detrimental to mind or body.

~ *Isaac Asimov*

All our final decisions are made in a state of mind that is not going to last.

~ *Marcel Proust*

There once was a time when all people believed in God and the church ruled. This time was called the Dark Ages.

~ *Richard Lederer*

A time has come when silence is betrayal. That time is now.

~ *Martin Luther King Jr.*

A long dispute means both parties are wrong.

~ *Voltaire*

Make your ego porous. Will is of little importance, complaining is nothing, fame is nothing. Openness, patience, receptivity, solitude is everything.

~ *Rainier Maria Rilke*

There are no facts, only interpretations.

~ *Nietzsche*

Life is life and fun is fun, but it is all so quiet when the goldfish dies.

~ *Translated from the Coptic*

The most detestable wickedness, the most horrid cruelties, and the greatest miseries that have afflicted the human race have had their origin in this thing called revelation, or revealed religion.

~ *Thomas Paine*

Don't clean our lenses; get the crack out of your own.

~ *Nothingarian slogan*

Our upside down welfare state is socialism for the rich, free enterprise for the poor. The great welfare scandal of the age concerns the dole we give rich people.

~ *William O. Douglas*

Humanity has advanced, when it has advanced, not because it has been sober, responsible, and cautious, but because it has been playful, rebellious, and immature.

~ *Tom Robbins*

Only a fool lets somebody else tell him who his enemy is.

~ *Assata Shakur*

The less you know, the more you think you know, because you don't know you don't know.

~ *Ray Stevens*

Friendships multiply joys and divide griefs.

~ *Henry G. Bohn*

The only reason for time is so that everything doesn't happen at once.

~ *Albert Einstein*

Some painters transform the sun into a yellow spot; others transform a yellow spot into the sun.

~ *Picasso*

Victorious warriors win first and then go to war, while defeated warriors go to war first and then seek to win.

~ *Sun tzu*

Do not worry. You have always written before and you will write now. All you have to do is write one true sentence. Write the truest sentence that you know.

~ *Hemingway*

We are drowning in information and starving for knowledge.

~ *Rutherford D. Roger*

I believe in God, only I spell it Nature.
~ *Frank Lloyd Wright*

Ours is a world of nuclear giants and ethical infants. We know more about war than we know about peace, more about killing that we know about living.
~ *Gen Omar N. Bradley*

I am not a liberator. Liberators do not exist. The people liberate themselves.
~ *Ernesto 'Che' Guevara*

Men will never be free until the last king is strangled with the entrails of the last priest.
~ *Denis Diderot*

You can't run away from your destiny, where you going to go?
~ *Theo Nast*

A dangerous path is this, like the edge of a razor.
~ *Hindu text*

The propaganda system allows the U.S. leadership to commit crimes without limit and with no suggestion of misbehavior or criminality; in fact, major war criminals like Henry Kissinger appear regularly on TV to comment on the crimes of the derivative butchers.
~ *Edward Herman*

Prisons are built with the stones of Law, brothels with the bricks of Religion.
~ *William Blake*

You, yourself, as much as anybody in the entire universe, deserve your love and affection.
~ *Buddha*

Can you sympathize with an exploding star?
~ *Shawn Mikula*

Those who make peaceful revolution impossible will make violent revolution inevitable.
~ *John F. Kennedy*

I distrust those people who know so well what God wants them to do because I notice it always coincides with their own desires.
~ *Susan B. Anthony*

If you understand everything, you must be misinformed.
~ *Japanese Proverb*

The revolution is a dictatorship of the exploited against the exploiters.
~ *Fidel Castro*

Whoever imagines himself a favorite with God holds others in contempt.
~ *Robert G. Ingersoll*

Forgiveness offers us a clean heart, and people will be one hundred times better after it.
~ *Mother Teresa*

When spider webs unite, they can tie up a lion.
~ *Ethiopian proverb*

Perfection of means and confusion of ends seem to characterize our age.
~ *Albert Einstein*

Simplicity is the ultimate sophistication.
~ *Leonardo da Vinci*

The ink of the scholar is holier than the blood of the martyr.

~ *Prophet Muhammad*

We don't live in the world of reality; we live in the world of how we perceive reality.

~ *Bryan Singer*

It has been my experience that folks who have no vices have very few virtues.

~ *Abraham Lincoln*

Let us so live that when we come to die even the undertaker will be sorry.

~ *Mark Twain*

There are many paths to the top of the mountain, but the view is always the same.

~ *Chinese Proverb*

The essence of knowledge is, having it, to apply it, not having it, to confess your ignorance.

~ *Confucius*

Few of us can easily surrender our belief that society must somehow make sense. The thought that the state has lost its mind and is punishing so many innocent people is intolerable. And so the evidence has to be internally denied.

~ *Arthur Miller*

The whole world is a man's birthplace.

~ *Caecilius Statius*

As far as I'm concerned, I prefer silent vice to ostentatious virtue.

~ *Albert Einstein*

Men never do evil so completely and cheerfully as when they do it from religious conviction.

~ *Blaise Pascal*

No one is entitled to the truth.

~ *E. Howard Hunt*

Question with boldness even the existence of a God; because, if there be one, he must more approve of the homage of reason, than that of blind folded fear.

~ *Thomas Jefferson*

It is good to have an end to journey toward, but it is the journey that matters in the end.

~ *Ursula K. LeGuin*

We are just statistics, born to consume resources.

~ *Horace*

If I had my child to raise all over again, I'd finger-paint more, and point the finger less. I would do less correcting and more connecting. I'd take my eyes off my watch, and watch with my eyes. I would care to know less, and know to care more. I'd take more hikes and fly more kites. I'd stop playing serious, and seriously play. I would run through more fields and gaze at more stars. I'd do more hugging and less tugging. I'd build self-esteem first, and the house later. I would be firm less often, and affirm much more. I'd teach less about the love of power, And more about the power of love.

~ *Diane Loomans*

Sometimes the test isn't finding the answer to a problem. It's seeing how you will react when you realize there are no answers.

~ *Unknown*

I hate and I love: why I do so you may well ask. I do not know, but I feel it happen and am in agony.

~ *Catullus*

Secrecy is the first essential in affairs of state.

~ *Cardinal Richelieu*

Wisdom oft lurks beneath a tattered coat.

~ *Caecilius Statius*

Conquest is easy. Control is not.

~ *James T. Kirk*

Only a life lived for others is a life worthwhile.

~ *Albert Einstein*

All religions are founded on the fear of the many and the cleverness of the few.

~ *Stendhal*

Character is what you are in the dark.

~ *Dwight L. Moody*

Religion is the brainchild of fear, and fear is the parent of cruelty. The greatest evils inflicted on humankind are perpetrated not by pleasure-seekers, self-seeking opportunists, or those who are merely amoral, but by fervent devotees of religion.

~ *Emmanuel Kofi Mensah*

You know your god is man-made when he hates all the same people you do.

~ *[Usenet]*

Today it is fashionable to talk about the poor. Unfortunately, it is not fashionable to talk with them.

~ *Mother Teresa*

I don't have to attend every argument I'm invited to.

~ *Unknown*

No man's knowledge here can go beyond his experience.

~ *John A. Locke*

Genuine poetry can communicate before it is understood.

~ *T. S. Eliot*

Next to a battle lost, the greatest misery is a battle gained.

~ *Duke of Wellington*

Be extremely subtle, even to the point of formlessness. Be extremely mysterious, even to the point of soundlessness. Thereby you can be the director of the opponent's fate.

~ *Sun tzu*

It's ok to look back at the past just don't stare at it.

~ *Unknown*

The animals you eat are not those who devour others; you do not eat the carnivorous beasts, you take them as your pattern. You only hunger after sweet and gentle creatures who harm no one, which follow you, serve you, and are devoured by you as the reward of their service.

~ *John Jacques Rousseau*

The reasonable man adjusts himself to the world, the unreasonable one persists in trying to adapt the world to himself; therefore all progress depends on the unreasonable man.

~ *George Bernard Shaw*

Life's under no obligation to give us what we expect.
~ *Margaret Mitchell*

The brook would lose its song if you removed the rocks.
~ *Fred Beck*

The world is governed more by appearances than realities, so that it is fully as necessary to seem to know something as to know it.
~ *Daniel Webster*

Nature acts without masters.
~ *Hippocrates*

The most dangerous thing is illusion.
~ *Ralph Waldo Emerson*

There is one thing stronger than all the armies in the world, and that is an idea whose time has come.
~ *Victor Hugo*

The notion that a radical is one who hates his country is naive and usually idiotic. He is, more likely, one who likes his country more than the rest of us, and is thus more disturbed than the rest of us when he sees it debauched. He is not a bad citizen turning to crime; he is a good citizen driven to despair.
~ *H. L. Mencken*

Character is made by what you stand for; reputation by what you fall for.
~ *Robert Quillen*

Talk not of wasted affection; affection never was wasted.
~ *Henry Wadsworth Longfellow*

Disobedience, in the eyes of anyone who has read history, is man's original virtue. It is through disobedience that progress has been made, through disobedience and through rebellion.

~ *Oscar Wilde*

It is amazing what you can accomplish if you do not care who gets the credit.

~ *Harry Truman*

The history of war is the history of powerful individuals willing to sacrifice thousands upon thousands of other people's lives for personal gains.

~ *Michael Rivero*

To live is not to learn, but to apply.

~ *Legouve*

Being with a woman all night never hurt no professional baseball player. It's staying up all night looking for a woman that does him in.

~ *Casey Stengel*

Do, or do not. There is no try.

~ *George Lucas*

The religion of the future will be a cosmic religion, the religion which based on experience, which refuses dogma.

~ *Albert Einstein*

Would you like to liberate yourself from the lower realms of life? Would you like to save the world from the degradation and destruction it seems destined for? Then step away from shallow mass movements and quietly go to work on your own self-awareness.

~ *Lao tzu*

It is curious that physical courage should be so common in the world and moral courage so rare.

~ *Mark Twain*

Hold a true friend with both hands.

~ *Nigerian Proverb*

Do not mind anything that anyone tells you about anyone else. Judge everyone and everything for yourself.

~ *Henry James*

When a thing has been said and said well, have no scruple. Take it and copy it.

~ *Anatole France*

The secret of happiness is to admire without desiring.

~ *F. H. Bradley*

Conversation would be vastly improved by the constant use of four simple words: I do not know.

~ *Andre Maurios*

To travel is to discover that everyone is wrong about other countries.

~ *Aldous Huxley*

Silence may be as variously shaded as speech.

~ *Edith Wharton*

The man who never alters his opinion is like standing water, he breeds reptiles of the mind.

~ *William Blake*

Pray: To ask the laws of the universe to be annulled on behalf of a single petitioner confessedly unworthy.

~ *Ambrose Bierce*

The Bible is not my book, and Christianity is not my religion. I could never give assent to the long, complicated statements of Christian dogma.

~ *Abraham Lincoln*

The greatest deception men suffer is from their own opinions.

~ *Leonardo da Vinci*

Anarchy is the only slight glimmer of hope.

~ *Mick Jagger*

We can lick gravity, but sometimes the paperwork is overwhelming.

~ *Wernher von Braun*

There is no ignorance outside the mind.

~ *Sankaracharya*

Tomorrow, and tomorrow, and tomorrow,
Creeps in this petty pace, from day to day,
To the last syllable of recorded time;
and all our yesterdays have lighted fools
the way to dusty death.

~ *William Shakespeare*

The gods are on the side of the stronger.

~ *Tacitus*

Do not be in a hurry to tie what you cannot untie.

~ *English Proverb*

Never let the fear of striking out get in your way.

~ *Babe Ruth*

A man can't be too careful in the choice of his enemies.

~ *Oscar Wilde*

Even if truth destroys the whole universe, still it is truth; stand by it.

~ *Swami Vivekananda*

A young monk traveled the road with an older priest. As they stopped at the roadside to rest and eat, the monk noticed the priest carried a mirror in his bag. Vanity, thought the monk. This old priest must keep the mirror to admire himself in secret. So he asked the priest why he carried the mirror, thinking surely he had caught him in a great sin. The old priest smiled and held the mirror up to the young monk's face. And the old priest said, I use the mirror in troubled times, to show me both the cause of my problems, and the solution. And so the young monk learned, like the old priest on his journey, that it is often wise when searching for the answer to your troubles, to look first at the face in the mirror.

~ *Old Chinese Story*

The actions of men are the best interpreters of their thoughts.

~ *John Locke*

A person reveals his character by nothing so clearly as the joke he resents.

~ *G. C. Lichtenberg*

Christians are supposed not merely to endure change, nor even to profit by it, but to cause it.

~ *Harry Emerson Fosdick*

We need lots of love to forgive. We need much more humility to ask for forgiveness.

~ *Mother Teresa*

Every man is guilty of all the good he didn't do.

~ *Voltaire*

Embrace all worldviews and perspectives, move beyond, and become enlightened. Kiss the stars and awaken to a new vision which is blinding at first, but your eyes will adjust, and you'll see the world, as it really is, for the first time.

~ *Shawn Mikula*

Take only memories; leave nothing but footprints.

~ *Chief Seattle*

Put your hand on a hot stove for a minute, and it seems like an hour. Sit with a pretty girl for an hour, and it seems like a minute. That's relativity.

~ *Albert Einstein*

Joy is not in things; it is in us.

~ *Richard Wagner*

If you would be a real seeker after truth, it is necessary that at least once in your life you doubt, as far as possible, all things.

~ *Rene Descartes*

Courage knows what not to fear.

~ *Socrates*

Anger manages everything badly.

~ *Slatius*

Time wounds all heels.

~ *Jane Ace*

Yesterday is but a dream and tomorrow is but a vision. But today, well-lived, makes every yesterday a dream of happiness, and every tomorrow a vision of hope, Live well, therefore, unto this day.

~ *Sanskrit proverb*

Making the decision to have a child is momentous. It's to decide forever to have your heart go walking around outside your body.

~ *Elizabeth Stone*

Poetry does not belong to those who wrote it, but to those who need it.

~ *Unknown*

Man is the only animal that blushes; or needs to.

~ *Mark Twain*

Beware of all enterprises that require new clothes.

~ *Henry David Thoreau*

If you can give something a name and a shape, you can have power over it. If it remains nameless and shapeless, it will continue to have power over you.

~ *Native American saying*

If people speak ill of you, live so that no one will believe them.

~ *Plato*

There is a "sanctity" involved with bringing a child into this world: it is better than bombing one out of it.

~ *James Baldwin*

Beauty is no quality in things themselves. It exists merely in the mind which contemplates them.

~ *David Hume*

Religion and nationalism is an invention useful to persuade men to murder each other for conveniently located lands without having to pay them what the job is worth.

~ *Michael Rivero*

Find compassion for others in your own transgressions.
~ *Gregg Krech*

The two most powerful warriors are patience and time.
~ *Leo Tolstoy*

Those with power and influence only feel themselves slowly sinking, and no matter how beautiful one's Titanic may be; the word unsinkable just makes the ocean hungry.
~ *David Wilcox*

Manifest plainness, embrace simplicity, reduce selfishness, have few desires.
~ *Lao tzu*

What if someone gave a war and nobody came? Life would ring the bells of ecstasy and forever be itself again.
~ *Allen Ginsberg*

You can either complain that rosebushes have thorns or rejoice that thorn bushes have roses.
~ *Unknown*

Can you run a country using courtesy and consideration? Then what more do you need? If you're incapable of running a country using courtesy and consideration, what good is your country?
~ *Confucius*

The dance is a poem of which each movement is a word.
~ *Mata Hari*

The pleasure of what we enjoy is lost by coveting more.
~ *Daniel Defoe*

Statistics are human beings with tears wiped off.
~ *Paul Brodeur*

When a man says he approves of something in principle, it means he hasn't the slightest intention of carrying it out in practice.
~ *Otto von Bismarck*

A man's character is his fate.
~ *Heraclitus*

Quarrels would not last long if only one side was wrong.
~ *Francois Duc de la Rochefoucauld*

Most history is just gossip that has grown old gracefully.
~ *Syndey J. Harris*

Philosophers have merely interpreted the world. The point is to change it.
~ *Karl Marx*

I am not a communist and neither is the revolutionary movement.
~ *Fidel Castro*

When a nation's young men are conservative, its funeral bell is already rung.
~ *Henry Ward Beecher*

Those who know how to think need no teachers.
~ *Mohandas Gandhi*

I did not know how to say goodbye. It was harder still, when I refused to say it.
~ *Native American saying*

Never was anything great achieved without danger.
~ *Niccolo Machiavelli*

Everyone likes to say Hitler did this and Hitler did that. But the truth is Hitler did very little. He was a world class asshole, but the evil actually done, from the death camps to World War Two, was all done by citizens who were afraid to question if what they were told by their government was the truth or not, and who because they did not want to admit to themselves that they were afraid to question the government, refused to see the truth behind the Reichstag Fire, refused to see the invasion by Poland was a staged fake, and followed Hitler into national disaster.
~ *Michael Rivero*

Every man takes the limits of his own field of vision for the limits of the world.
~ *Arthur Schopenhauer*

Science is the great antidote to the poison of enthusiasm and superstition.
~ *Adam Smith*

Beauty is not in the face; beauty is a light in the heart.
~ *Kahil Gilbran*

A noble thought is a prayer. An earnest desire is a prayer. A pious longing is a prayer. The sincere sighing of a penitent heart is a prayer.
~ *Zarathushtra*

The Brush Dance is a Yurok healing ritual where being true to yourself means give your best to a person in need. Being true to yourself is the one and only Yurok Indian Law.
~ *Brush Dance Journal*

The optimist claims that we live in the best of all possible worlds. The pessimist fears this true.

~ *James Branch Cabell*

You win a few, you lose a few. Some get rained out. But you got to dress for all of them.

~ *Satchel Paige*

We have a criminal jury system, which is superior to any in the world; and its efficiency is only marred by the difficulty of finding twelve men every day who don't know anything and can't read.

~ *Mark Twain*

Happiness is an imaginary condition, formerly attributed by the living to the dead, now usually attributed by adults to children, and by children to adults.

~ *Thomas Szasz*

I believe that religion, generally speaking, has been a curse to mankind.

~ *H. L. Mencken*

Never explain, your friends do not need it and your enemies will not believe you anyway.

~ *Elbert Hubbard*

If a woman has to choose between catching a fly ball and saving an infant's life, she will choose to save the infant's life without even considering if there are men on base.

~ *Dave Barry*

The pious pretense that evil does not exist only makes it vague, enormous and menacing.

~ *Aleister Crowley*

A boy handed his father a poor report card, he asked, ‘Dad, what do you think my trouble is, heredity or environment?’

~ *Unknown*

I know God won't give me anything I can't handle. I just wish he didn't trust me so much.

~ *Mother Teresa*

Once all struggle is grasped, miracles are possible.

~ *Mao Tse Tung*

Everybody sooner or later, sits down to a banquet of consequences.

~ *Robert Louis Stevenson*

No man is justified in doing evil on the grounds of expediency.

~ *Theodore Roosevelt*

You may make mistakes, but you are not a failure until you start blaming someone else.

~ *Unknown*

The only purpose for which power can be rightfully exercised over any member of a civilized community, against his will, is to prevent harm to others. His own good, either physical or moral, is not a sufficient warrant.

~ *John Stuart Mill*

He who asks is a fool for five minutes, but he who does not ask remains a fool forever.

~ *Old Chinese saying*

We will be known by the tracks we leave behind.

~ *Dakota proverb*

If a scholar aspires to the Way but is ashamed of bad clothes and bad food, he isn't ready to join the discussion yet.

~ *Confucius*

Earth provides enough to satisfy every man's need, but not every man's greed.

~ *Mohandas Gandhi*

Peace and friendship with all mankind is our wisest policy, and I wish we may be permitted to pursue it.

~ *Thomas Jefferson*

I myself have never been able to find out precisely what feminism is; I only know that people call me a feminist whenever I express sentiments that differentiate me from a doormat or a prostitute.

~ *Rebecca West*

The Wright Brothers weren't the first to fly. They were just the first not to crash.

~ *Unknown*

...so long as the media are in corporate hands, the task of social change will be vastly more difficult, if not impossible.

~ *Robert McChesney*

It is wrong always, everywhere, and for anyone, to believe anything upon insufficient evidence.

~ *William Kingdon Clifford*

What is the difference between unethical and ethical advertising? Unethical advertising uses falsehoods to deceive the public; ethical advertising uses truth to deceive the public.

~ *Vilhjalmur Stefansson*

I do not believe that any type of religion should ever be introduced into the public schools of the United States.

~ *Thomas Edison*

Thank you for touching me. Some of the only moments worth living were spent with you. Not you especially, the collective you.

~ *Henry Rollins*

The radical invents the views. When he has worn them out, the conservative adopts them.

~ *Mark Twain*

You can lead a boy to college, but you cannot make him think.

~ *Elbert Hubbard*

A bishop keeps on saying at the age of eighty what he was told to say at the age of eighteen.

~ *Oscar Wilde*

That which is static and repetitive is boring. That which is dynamic and random is confusing. In between lies art.

~ *John A. Locke*

Overcome anger by non-anger, overcome evil by good. Overcome the miser by giving, overcome the liar by truth.

~ *Dhammapada*

Examinations consist of the foolish asking questions the wise cannot answer.

~ *Oscar Wilde*

If I had my life to live over again, I'd be a plumber.

~ *Albert Einstein*

Monarchy degenerates into tyranny, aristocracy into oligarchy, and democracy into savage violence and chaos.

~ *Polybius*

Experience teaches us to be most on our guard to protect liberty when the government's purposes are beneficent.

~ *Louis Brandeis*

Stopping terrorism is simple. Just quit screwing around with other people's countries and the terrorists will go home. But the government of the United States wants to go on screwing around with other people's countries, refuses to stop, indeed views it as Manifest Destiny for the United States Government to persist in screwing around with other people's countries, and views the inconvenience, increased tax burden, loss of civil liberties, and even deaths among the American people as just another cost of doing business.

~ *Michael Rivero*

I've imagined great victories, and I've imagined great races. The races are better.

~ *Mark Helprin*

Never interrupt your enemy when he is making a mistake.

~ *Napoleon*

The love of one's country is a splendid thing. But why should love stop at the border?

~ *Pablo Casals*

When the water starts boiling it is foolish to turn off the heat.

~ *Nelson Mandela*

You should not suffer the past. You should be able to wear it like a loose garment, take it off and let it drop.

~ *Eva Jessye*

Everything that we are is the result of what we have thought.

~ *Buddha*

I may not be totally perfect, but parts of me are excellent.

~ *Ashleigh Brilliant*

I am a Marxist Leninist and I will be one until the last day of my life.

~ *Fidel Castro*

The spirit of resistance to government is so valuable on certain occasions that I wish it to be always kept alive.

~ *Thomas Jefferson*

If we continue to develop our technology without wisdom or prudence, our servant may prove to be our executioner.

~ *General Omar N. Bradley*

The rights of women are sacred. See that women are maintained in the rights attributed to them.

~ *Prophet Muhammed*

Try not to become a man of success but rather to become a man of value.

~ *Albert Einstein*

When you meet a worthy person, focus on reaching his level. When you meet an unworthy person, take a good look inside yourself.

~ *Confucius*

I do not feign hypotheses.
~ *Sir Isaac Newton*

I find the great thing in this world is not so much where we stand, as in what direction we are moving. We must sail sometimes with the wind and sometimes against it. But we must sail, and not drift, nor lie at anchor.
~ *Oliver Wendell Holmes*

Know thy lot, know thine enemies, and know thyself.
~ *Sun tzu*

In all the disputes, which have excited Christians against each other, Rome has invariably decided in favor of that opinion which tended most towards the suppression of the human intellect and the annihilation of the reasoning powers.
~ *Voltaire*

There is another man within me that's angry with me.
~ *Sir Thomas Browne*

For three days after death, hair and fingernails continue to grow but phone calls taper off.
~ *Johnny Carson*

If one were to take the bible seriously one would go mad. But to take the bible seriously, one must be already mad.
~ *Aleister Crowley*

Although the world is full of suffering, it is also full of the overcoming of it.
~ *Helen Keller*

The only abnormality is the incapacity to love.
~ *Anaïs Nin*

All my humor is based upon destruction and despair. If the whole world were tranquil, without disease and violence, I'd be standing on the breadline right in back of J. Edgar Hoover.

~ *Lenny Bruce*

If poetry comes not as naturally as the leaves to a tree, it better not come at all.

~ *John Keats*

The meeting of two personalities is like the contact of two chemical substances; if there is any reaction, both are transformed.

~ *Carl Gustav Jung*

There is no conversation more boring than the one where everybody agrees.

~ *Michel de Montaigne*

I do not pray. I do not expect God to single me out and grant me advantages over my fellow men. Prayer seems to me a cry of weakness, and an attempt to avoid, by trickery, the rules of the game as laid down. I do not choose to admit weakness. I accept the challenge of responsibility.

~ *Zora Neale Houston*

History is the version of past events that people have decided to agree upon.

~ *Napoleon*

How many things can I do without!

~ *Socrates*

If I can't dance, I don't want to be part of your revolution.

~ *Emma Goldman*

It is not what we do, but also what we do not do, for which we are accountable.

~ *Moliere*

Kind words can be short and easy to speak, but their echoes are truly endless.

~ *Mother Teresa*

Religion is excellent stuff for keeping common people quiet.

~ *Napoleon*

The only stable state is the one in which all men are equal before the law.

~ *Aristotle*

The modern liberal state ... often uses deception to gain its ends, not so much deception of the foreign enemy, but of its own citizens, who have been taught to trust their leaders.

~ *Howard Zinn*

He who controls the past commands the future. He who commands the future conquers the past.

~ *George Orwell*

Where observation is concerned, chance favors only the prepared mind.

~ *Louis Pasteur*

I shall never be ashamed of citing a bad author if the line is good.

~ *Seneca*

Perhaps I know why it is man alone who laughs: He alone suffers so deeply that he had to invent laughter.

~ *Nietzsche*

It was, of course, a lie what you read about my religious convictions, a lie which is being systematically repeated. I do not believe in a personal god and I have never denied this but have expressed it clearly. If something is in me which can be called religious, then it is the unbounded admiration for the structure of the world so far as our science can reveal it.

~ *Albert Einstein*

Living is change; Growth is optional.

~ *Juan Wa Chang*

It is difficult to produce a television documentary that is both incisive and probing when every twelve minutes one is interrupted by twelve dancing rabbits singing about toilet paper.

~ *Rod Serling*

You have not converted a man because you have silenced him.

~ *John Morley*

We have a political system that awards office to the most ruthless, cunning, and selfish of mortals, then act surprised when those willing to do anything to win power are equally willing to do anything with it.

~ *Michael Rivero*

The notes I handle no better than many pianists. But the pauses between the notes, ahh, that is where the art resides!

~ *Arthur Schnabel*

The democrats say they are gonna screw you and they screw you. The republicans say they aren't gonna screw you and they screw you.

~ *Unknown*

Many people in the world are independent, but very few are free.

~ *J. Krishnamurthi*

Use what talent you possess: the woods would be very silent if no birds sang except those that sang best.

~ *Henry Van Dyke*

All great truths begin as blasphemies.

~ *George Bernard Shaw*

O Lord, help me to be pure, but not yet.

~ *Saint Augustine*

Good humor is one of the best articles of dress one can wear in society.

~ *William Makepeace Thackeray*

What difference does it make to the dead, the orphans, and the homeless, whether the mad destruction is wrought under the name of totalitarianism or the holy name of liberty and democracy?

~ *Mohandas Gandhi*

The hardest years in life are those between ten and seventy.

~ *Helen Hayes, age 83*

The Democrats are the party of government activism, the party that says government can make you richer, smarter, taller, and get the chickweed out of your lawn. Republicans are the party that says government doesn't work, and then gets elected and proves it.

~ *P. J. O'Rourke*

Everything has been figured out, except how to live.

~ *Jean Paul Sartre*

There was a time when I believed in the story and the scheme of salvation, so far as I could understand it, just as I believed there was a Devil. Suddenly the light broke through to me and I saw a silly story, and each generation nowadays swallows it with greater difficulty. Why do people go on pretending about this Christianity?

~ *H. G. Wells*

The enemy isn't conservatism. The enemy isn't liberalism. The enemy is bullshit.

~ *Lars-Erik Nelson*

The vast majority of mankind is trapped within perceptual prisons.

~ *Shawn Mikula*

It does not require a majority to prevail, but rather an irate, tireless minority keen to set brush fires in people's minds.

~ *Samuel Adams*

Religion is an insult to human dignity. With or without it, you'd have good people doing good things and evil people doing bad things, but for good people to do bad things, it takes religion.

~ *Steven Weinberg*

What difference does it make how much you have? What you do not have amounts to much more.

~ *Seneca*

America ... just a nation of two hundred million used car salesmen with all the money we need to buy guns and no qualms about killing anybody else in the world who tries to make us uncomfortable.

~ *Hunter S. Thompson*

The government of the United States does not, in its policies, express the decency of its people.

~ *Jerry Fresia*

Grasshopper, look beyond the game, as you look beneath the surface of the pool to see its depths.

~ *Master Po*

It is only with the heart that one can see rightly; what is essential is invisible to the eye.

~ *Antoine De Saint*

Write injuries in sand, kindnesses in marble.

~ *French proverb*

I pray every single second of my life; not on my knees but with my work. My prayer is to lift women to equality with men. Work and worship are one with me. I know there is no God of the universe made happy by my getting down on my knees and calling him 'great.'

~ *Susan B. Anthony*

Kindness is a mark of faith, and whoever has not kindness has not faith.

~ *Prophet Muhammad*

Ah, the future! That period of time in which our affairs prosper, our friends are true and our happiness is assured.

~ *Ambrose Bierce*

Where we have strong emotions, we're liable to fool ourselves.

~ *Carl Sagan*

Call on God, but row away from the rocks.

~ *Indian proverb*

Everybody's worried about stopping terrorism. Well, there's a really easy way; stop participating in it.

~ *Noam Chomsky*

It is part of the general pattern of misguided policy that our country is now geared to an arms economy which was bred in an artificially induced psychosis of war hysteria and nurtured upon an incessant propaganda of fear.

~ *General Douglas MacArthur*

To fear love is to fear life, and those who fear life are already three parts dead.

~ *Bertrand Russell*

We've got to pause and ask ourselves, how much clean air do we need?

~ *Lee Iacocca*

Every situation, nay, every moment, is of infinite worth, for it is the representative of a whole eternity.

~ *Johann Wolfgang von Goethe*

Everyone laughs and cries in the same language.

~ *dreamslaughter*

We all need to keep our feet on the ground but some will reach for the stars.

~ *<maggijo>*

The height of cleverness is to be able to conceal it.

~ *Francois Duc de la Rochefoucauld*

I never would have agreed to the formulation of the Central Intelligence Agency back in forty-seven, if I had known it would become the American Gestapo.

~ *Harry S Truman, 1961*

Art is a lie that makes us realize the truth.
~ *Pablo Picasso*

Why of course the people don't want war. Why should some poor slob on a farm want to risk his life in a war when the best he can get out of it is to come back to his farm in one piece? Naturally, the common people don't want war; neither in Russia, nor in England, nor for that matter in Germany. That is understood. But after all, it is the leaders of the country who determine the policy, and it is always a simple matter to drag the people along, whether it is a democracy, or a fascist dictatorship, or a parliament, or a communist dictatorship... Voice or no voice, the people can always be brought to the bidding of the leaders. That is easy. All you have to do is to tell them they are being attacked, and denounce the pacifists for lack of patriotism and exposing the country to danger.
~ *Nazi Hermann Goering*

The difference between our decadence and the Russians' is that while theirs is brutal, ours is apathetic.
~ *James Thurber*

Beauty is the promise of happiness.
~ *Stendhal*

Example has more followers than reason.
~ *Christian Bovee*

A revolution is not a bed of roses. A revolution is a struggle between the future and the past.
~ *Fidel Castro*

It is not impossible to govern Italians. It is merely useless.
~ *Benito Mussolini*

You are remembered for the rules you break.

~ *Douglas MacArthur*

Invisible Pink Unicorns are beings of awesome mystical power. We know this because they manage to be invisible and pink at the same time. Like all religions, the Faith of the Invisible Pink Unicorns is based upon both logic and faith. We have faith that they are pink; we logically know that they are invisible because we can't see them.

~ *Steve Eley*

There must be more to life than having everything.

~ *Maurice Sendak*

Holding on to anger is like holding on to a hot coal with the intent of throwing it at someone else; you are the one who gets burned.

~ *Buddha*

Only two things are infinite, the universe and human stupidity, and I'm not sure about the former.

~ *Albert Einstein*

If one acknowledges a group or a nation willing to commit atrocities, then one must also acknowledges the existence of a nation willing to commit atrocities to blame on the first nation.

~ *Michael Rivero*

Excess on occasion is exhilarating. It prevents moderation from acquiring the deadening effect of a habit.

~ *William Somerset Maugham*

There is more to life than increasing its speed.

~ *Mohandas Gandhi*

Every revolution evaporates and leaves behind it only the slime of bureaucracy.

~ *Franz Kafka*

Always remember you are a totally unique individual; just like everyone else.

~ *Unknown*

Because I do it with one small ship, I am called a terrorist. You do it with a whole fleet and are called an emperor.

~ *St. Augustine*

Mythology is what we call someone else's religion.

~ *Joseph Campbell*

Love gives us in a moment what we can hardly attain by years of toil.

~ *Johann Wolfgang von Goethe*

Someday man will imprison the power of the sun, release atomic power, and harness the rise and fall of the tides. I am proud of the fact that I never invented weapons to kill.

~ *Thomas Edison*

The only thing we never get enough of is love; and the only thing we never give enough of is love.

~ *Henry Miller*

Blood alone moves the wheels of history.

~ *Benito Mussolini*

... The biggest detractors of communism and socialism always seem to want to embrace the worst excesses of both.

~ *<Skullhunter>*

Beware the man of one book.

~ *Saint Thomas Aquinas*

Half of life is fucking up; the other half is dealing with it.

~ *Henry Rollins*

Victory attained by violence is tantamount to a defeat, for it is momentary.

~ *Mohandas Gandhi*

If we don't believe in freedom of expression for people we despise, we don't believe in it at all.

~ *Noam Chomsky*

Unless Americans come to realize that they are not stronger in the world because they have the bomb but weaker because of their vulnerability to atomic attack, they are not likely to conduct their policy, in a spirit that furthers the arrival at an understanding.

~ *Albert Einstein*

The establishment of Christianity arrested the normal development of the physical sciences for over fifteen hundred years.

~ *Andrew Dickson White*

If god created us in his image we have certainly returned the compliment.

~ *Voltaire*

The mere act of believing that some wrongful course of action constitutes an advantage is pernicious.

~ *Marcus Tullius Cicero*

The hunger for love is much more difficult to remove than the hunger for bread.

~ *Mother Teresa*

The United States is not nearly so concerned that its acts be kept secret from its intended victims as it is that the American people not know of them.

~ *Ramsey Clark*

Nothing exists except atoms and empty space; everything else is opinion.

~ *Democritus*

As with the Christian religion, the worst advertisement for Socialism is its adherents.

~ *George Orwell*

There is enough for man's need but not for man's greed.

~ *Mohandas Gandhi*

Every war when it comes, or before it comes, is represented not as a war but as an act of self-defense against a homicidal maniac.

~ *George Orwell*

Disobedience is the true foundation of liberty. The obedient must be slaves.

~ *Henry David Thoreau*

The first evil of those who are prone to talk, is that they hear nothing.

~ *Plutarch*

Cancel the kitchen scraps for lepers and orphans! No more merciful beheadings! And call off Christmas!

~ *The Sheriff of Nottingham*

No great discovery was ever made without a bold guess.

~ *Isaac Newton*

The invisible and the non-existent look very much alike.
~ *Delos B. McKown*

Reporter: What do you think of Western civilization?
Mohandas Gandhi: I think it would be a good idea.

The god of the cannibals will be a cannibal, of the crusaders, a crusader, and of the merchants a merchant.
~ *Ralph Waldo Emerson*

The degree of one's emotion varies inversely with one's knowledge of the facts. The less you know, the hotter you get.
~ *Bertrand Russel*

It is dangerous to be sincere unless you are also stupid.
~ *George Bernard Shaw*

Why do the people think so little of death? Because the rulers demand too much of life; therefore the people take death lightly.
~ *Lao tzu*

I came to America because of the great, great freedom which I heard existed in this country. I made a mistake in selecting America as a land of freedom, a mistake I cannot repair in the balance of my lifetime.
~ *Albert Einstein*

There is nothing worse than aggressive stupidity.
~ *Johann Wolfgang von Goethe*

This would be the best of all possible worlds, if there were no religion in it.
~ *John Adams*

Do not fear to be eccentric in opinion, for every opinion now accepted was once eccentric.

~ *Bertrand Russell*

If Christ were here now there is one thing he would not be, a Christian.

~ *Mark Twain*

Knowing others is intelligence; knowing yourself is true wisdom. Mastering others is strength; mastering yourself is true power.

~ *Lao Tzu*

The majority cannot reason; it has no judgment. It has always placed its destiny in the hands of others; it has followed its leaders even into destruction. The mass has always opposed, condemned, and hounded the innovator, the pioneer of a new truth.

~ *Emma Goldman*

Men who believe absurdities will commit atrocities.

~ *Voltaire*

It is poverty to decide that a child must die so that you may live as you wish.

~ *Mother Teresa*

To read a newspaper is to refrain from reading something worthwhile. The first discipline of education must therefore be to refuse resolutely to feed the mind with canned chatter.

~ *Aleister Crowley*

The growth of wisdom may be gauged exactly by the diminution of ill temper.

~ *Nietzsche*

Your every decision conspires to make this moment happen.

~ *Christi Philpott*

Yes, my friends, I too am prepared to die for a cause, but there is no cause for which I am prepared to kill.

~ *Mohandas Gandhi*

We, on our side, are praying to Him to give us victory, because we believe we are right; but those on the other side pray to Him, too, for victory, believing they are right. What must He think of us?

~ *Abraham Lincoln*

A time will come when a politician who has willfully made war and promoted international dissension will be ... surer of the noose than a private homicide.

~ *H. G. Wells*

The Church says that the earth is flat, but I know that it is round, for I have seen the shadow on the moon, and I have more faith in a shadow than in the Church.

~ *Ferdinand Magellan*

I'm gonna share with you a vision that I had, cause I love you. And you feel it. You know all that money we spend on nuclear weapons and defense each year, trillions of dollars, correct? Instead, just play with this, if we spent that money feeding and clothing the poor of the world, and it would pay for it many times over, not one human being excluded. We can explore space together, both inner and outer, forever in peace. Thank you very much. You're great, I hope you enjoyed it.

~ *Bill Hicks*

Death Bed

I should never have switched from Scotch to Martinis.
~ *Humphrey Bogart*

Too late for fruit, too soon for flowers.
~ *Walter De La Mare*

I wonder why he shot me.
~ *Huey P. Long Jr.*

Is this dying? Is this all? Is this what I feared when I prayed against a hard death? Oh, I can bear this! I can bear this!
~ *Cotton Mather*

Give me eighty men and I'll ride through the whole Sioux nation.
~ *William J. Fetterman*

Lord help my poor soul.
~ *Edgar Allan Poe*

It is finished.
~ *Jesus of Nazareth, John 19:30*

My God, my God, why have you forsaken me!?
~ *Jesus of Nazareth, Mark 15:34-5, Matthew 27:46*

Father, into thy hands I commend my spirit.
~ *Jesus of Nazareth, Luke 23:46*

Don't let it end like this. Tell them I said something.
~ *Francisco 'Poncho' Villa*

God damn the whole friggin' world and everyone in it but you, Carlotta.
~ *W. C. Fields*

God bless ... God damn.
~ *James Thurber*

KHAQQ calling Itasca. We must be on you, but cannot see you. Gas is running low.
~ *Amelia Earhart*

Go on, get out! Last words are for fools who haven't said enough.
~ *Karl Marx*

How were the circus receipts in Madison Square Gardens?
~ *Phineas Taylor Barnum*

Now comes the mystery.
~ *Henry Ward Beecher*

Friends applaud, the comedy is over.
~ *Ludwig van Beethoven*

Strike the tent.
~ *Robert E. Lee*

Dying is easy. Comedy is difficult.
~ *Edmund Gwenn*

I have offended God and mankind because my work did not reach the quality it should have.
~ *Leonardo da Vinci*

They couldn't hit an elephant at this dist ...
~ *General John Sedgwick*

Curtain! Fast music! Lights! Ready for the last finale! Great! The show looks good. The show looks good.

~ *Ziegfeld Florenz*

Tell mother; tell mother, I died for my country ... Useless ... useless ...

~ *John Wilkes Booth*

I've had eighteen straight whiskies; I think that's the record.

~ *Dylan Thomas*

Who is it?

~ *Billy the Kid*

Leave the shower curtain on the inside of the tub.

~ *Conrad N. Hilton*

I owe much; I have nothing; the rest I leave to the poor.

~ *François Rabelais*

Do you know where I can get any shit?

~ *Lenny Bruce*

Is it the Fourth?

~ *Thomas Jefferson*

Let's cool it brothers.

~ *Malcolm X*

I feel nothing, apart from a certain difficulty in continuing to exist.

~ *Bernard de Fontenelle*

I knew it. I knew it; born in a hotel room, and God damn it, died in a hotel room.

~ *Eugene O'Neill*

You too, Brutus?

~ *Julius Caesar*

Hold the cross high so I may see it through the flames!

~ *Saint Joan of Arc*

Turn me. I am roasted on one side.

~ *Saint Lawrence*

Why not? Yeah.

~ *Timothy Leary*

I see black light.

~ *Victor Hugo*

God will pardon me, that's his line of work.

~ *Heinrich Heine*

I do not have to forgive my enemies. I have had them all shot.

~ *Ramon Maria Narvaez*

That was a great game of golf, fellers.

~ *Bing Crosby*

It is very beautiful over there.

~ *Thomas Edison*

Tomorrow, I shall no longer be here.

~ *Nostradamus*

Has God forgotten everything I've done for him?

~ *Louis XIV*

I've had a hell of a lot of fun and I've enjoyed every minute of it.

~ *Errol Flynn*

A dying man can do nothing easy.
~ *Ben Franklin*

I am about to, or I am going to, die: either expression is correct.
~ *Dominique Bouhours, French grammarian*

Here am I, dying of a hundred good symptoms.
~ *Alexander Pope*

Capital punishment: Them without the capital get the punishment.
~ *John Spenkelink*

How about this for a headline? French Fries.
~ *James French*

Why yes, a bullet proof vest.
~ *James Roges*

Well, gentlemen, you are about to see a baked apple.
~ *George Appel*

I want to live because there are a few things I still want to do.
~ *Aneurin Bevan*

I am about to take my last voyage, a great leap in the dark.
~ *René Descartes*

There are no more other worlds to conquer!
~ *Alexander the Great*

Damn it ... Don't you dare ask God to help me.
~ *Joan Crawford*

I'm bored with it all.

~ *Winston Churchill*

Thomas Jefferson still survives.

~ *John Adams*

We are all full of weakness and errors; let us mutually pardon each other our follies it is the first law of nature.

~ *Voltaire*

I did not know that we had ever quarreled.

~ *Henry David Thoreau, when asked to make peace with God*

Doctor, I die hard, but I am not afraid to go.

~ *George Washington*

Ah, Luisa, you always arrive just as I am leaving.

~ *Massimo Taparelli Azeglio*

Either this wallpaper goes, or I do!

~ *Oscar Wilde*

That was the best ice-cream soda I ever tasted.

~ *Lou Costello*

I'll bet in Heaven they have one single word that means 'back when I was alive'. You know, to save time in meetings and stuff.

~ *Derek Littlefield*

Goodnight my darlings, I'll see you tomorrow.

~ *Noel Coward*

Thank you.

~ *Laura Jane Moore*

Most of these quotes should be close to correct, but we're only human and who knows what to believe anymore. Please, take these quotes for the intent and meaning and not for the absolute historical accuracy.

Any corrections will be appreciated.

Suggestions for 'Burn This Book Too' can be sent to:

http://www.dreamslaughter.com

Michael Keyes

Keira Bossung

Christi Philpott

Michael Flattery

Gary Zietlow

Dru Abel

Mrs. B

David R. Fisher

Colby French

Keion Moradi

Jeffrey Abel

Theo Nast

Margaret Jones

Lance Bradley

Kelly Philpott

David Keyes

Rachelle Whaley

Daniel Keyes

Daryl Suzanne Stutley

http://newsgarden.org